No Longer Property of
Phillips Memorial Library

D1316167

TOMORROW'S CHURCH

What's Ahead for
American Catholics

TOMORROW'S CHURCH

What's Ahead for American Catholics

edited by
Edward C. Herr

THE THOMAS MORE PRESS
Chicago, Illinois

PHILLIPS MEMORIAL
LIBRARY
PROVIDENCE COLLEGE

BX
1390
T65
1982

Copyright © 1982 by the Thomas More Association. All rights reserved. Printed in the United States of America. No part of this publication may be reproduced, stored in a retrieval system, or transmitted, in any form or by any means, electronic, mechanical, photocopying, recording, or otherwise, without the written permission of the publisher, The Thomas More Association, 225 W. Huron St., Chicago, Illinois 60610.

ISBN 0-88347-137-X

CONTENTS

Contributors

KAYE ASHE, O.P., is Associate Dean of Rosary College, River Forest, Ill., has written for *The Critic* magazine and is at work on a book about the modern Catholic woman which will be published in 1983 by the Thomas More Press.

CYPRIAN DAVIS, O.S.B., is professor of Church History in the St. Meinrad Archabbey School of Theology. He received his doctorate in history from the Louvain in Belgium in 1977 and was a founding member of the Black Catholic Clergy Caucus in 1968. Father Davis has written several articles for the *New Catholic Encyclopedia* and *America* and is the author of a high school history text *The Church: A Living History* (Silver Burdett)

MARY G. DURKIN, a pastoral theologian, has a Doctor of Ministry degree from the Divinity School of the University of Chicago. She has worked extensively in adult religious education in the areas of theology, marriage and family life and sexuality. She is author of *The Suburban Woman: Her Changing Role in the Church* and is co-author of *A Catholic Perspec-*

tive: Divorce and *Marital Intimacy: A Catholic Perspective* as well as a contributor to the study and book *Parish, Priest and People.*

JOHN GARVEY, critic and frequent contributor to *Commonweal*, is the author of *Saints for Confused Times* and co-author of *Catholic Perspectives: Abortion.*

ANDREW GREELEY, sociologist, syndicated columnist, and novelist, is the author of more than 80 books and has, as a senior project director at the National Opinion Research Center, headed up many important sociological studies of American Catholic life.

EDWARD C. HERR, a priest of the Diocese of Toledo, Ohio, has spent 43 years in Catholic education as teacher and principal. Since his retirement in 1980, he has edited OVERVIEW, a monthly newsletter, for the Thomas More Association. Three of his cassettes are also distributed by the Association: "Are Parents Afraid of Their Teen-Agers?"; "To Teen-Agers/on Sex/With Love" and "The Sacrament of Confession: Alienation or Reconciliation?"

JAMES HITCHCOCK, Professor of History at St. Louis University, is the author of a number of books including *The Recovery of the Sacred, Catholicism and Modernity, The Decline and Fall of Radical Catholicism* and the just published *The New Enthusiasts and What They Are Doing to the Catholic Church.*

THOMAS A. KLEISSLER is Director of the Office of Pastoral Renewal of the Archdiocese of Newark, New Jersey. Out of his many years experience in both urban and suburban parishes, Monsignor Kleissler directs and played a founding role in RENEW, a parish spiritual renewal program now active in some 25 dioceses.

MARTIN E. MARTY is Fairfax M. Cone Distinguished Service Professor of the History of Modern Christianity at the University of Chicago, associate editor of *The Christian Century*, author of the newsletter CONTEXT, a National Book Award winner and author of many books, including the new *The Public Church: Mainline-Evangelical-Catholic.*

FRANK PONCE, Associate Director and Research Assistant, Secretariat for Hispanic Affairs, National Conference of Bishops, Washington, D.C., is a priest of the Diocese of San Bernardino, California. Ordained in 1972, Father Ponce has a Ph.D. from Stanford University and travels extensively to maintain close ties with and to research the needs of Hispanics. He developed the "Communidades Eclesiales de Base (CEB)" as a method of focusing on evangelization and community formation.

FOREWORD

IF, as Santayana has warned, those who ignore history are doomed to repeat it, what risks do we run if we fail to look ahead, if we make no effort to prepare for the future? Living our lives one day at a time is said by some to be conducive to mental health but I suspect that this advice is sound only for individuals, not for groups, institutions or societies. Most would agree, I think, that it is worth planning the kind of environment we will live in even if as individuals we might have developed the capacity to go with the flow, to sustain life's brief candle even when confronted with the harsh breath arising from a worst possible environmental scenario.

Limning the future, of course, is not for the faint hearted. It demands, among other things, that the prognosticator have the nerves of a river boat gambler. It is of little use to predict that on the one hand things may be this way while on the other hand they may be that way. A choice must be made. The arrow marking the trail must, say, point northwest or northeast. It can't say either or both. But while we recognize that reading today's tea leaves to predict tomorrow's life is terribly difficult, we have no choice but to insist now on internal credibility in the predictions made. I think the reader will find such internal credibility in *Tomorrow's Church*.

Predicting accurately the future of a vast, amorphous entity such as the Catholic Church would seem to be especially difficult. Not only is the Church made up of millions of individuals from dozens of cultures, widely variegated in age and education but its leaders range from brilliant and inspiring to pedestrian and dull. Not only must the futurologist be in command of a computer of almost infinite flexibility, he or she must face up to the fact that Catholics believe that God will always be with the church and that the Holy Spirit will blow where He or She will.

The authors of the chapters of *Tomorrow's Church* are not always in agreement. This is not surprising because their points of departure vary from the traditional to the progressive, from conservative to liberal. But all, it is apparent, are unswerving in their devotion to the Church. And all, if not always optimistic, are hopeful as they look to its future. But despite the varying orientation of the book's contributors, none of them is giddily euphoric in sketching a future in which all today's structures are replaced and all today's problems are solved.

Most, I think, would agree with contributor James Hitchcock that "nothing now seems as dated as those imaginative projections of the future sketched out by optimists of fifty or seventy-five years ago." They would agree too with Hitchcock that "not only has such a future not been realized . . . but relatively few people would now want it. Not only do we find much of the past worth saving . . . but we question the cost —in energy, in use of material, in alienation from nature—which would make such a life possible."

But it would be naive not to realize that the dynamics of the second Vatican Council have not ceased to reverberate. They may, in fact, have only begun to be felt. The charge that Pope John gave to the bishops assembled for the Council took their breath away: "The truths of the faith are one thing. How they are explained is another." No wonder that some of the Council reactionaries accused the pope, privately of course, of heresy. These defenders of the status quo saw no reason for change. They liked things exactly as they were. The motto of one of them was "Semper Idem," always the same. The tide that Pope John engendered continues to ebb and flow and it seems unlikely that it will subside in the foreseeable future.

The contributors to *Tomorrow's Church* look ahead to the parish, the priesthood, the laity and the Catholic schools of the future. The role of women, blacks and Hispanics is projected as is the way in which future church will address "the task of providing a vision of marriage that will encourage people to make an effort at working at marital intimacy." Finally, the always perceptive Martin E. Marty looks at the future of relations between Catholics on the one hand and Protestants and Jews on the other.

In his view Dr. Marty points up the magnitude of this book's scope. "The gap in perceptions," he writes, "between the coming generation, the American majority, which has not a trace of memory of pre-Vatican II Catholicism and our generation, which saw the great transition, is awesome. Whoever looks ahead to tomorrow's Catholicism has to keep in mind how much can happen in one generation, or, as we learned between 1958 and 1965, in a seven year span."

Looked at from another vantage point we realize that a Catholic who today has reached age 55, the age of passage into "senior" citizenship, was but 35 when the Council began and 38 when it ended. This middle group has been in the thick of the yeasting that has been taking place and there is no reason to believe that they, in the years ahead, will be a drag against the continued questing and restoring of their presumably more vibrant younger generations.

In any event, commentators today and those looking into the crystal ball of *Tomorrow's Church* seem to see the Vatican Council's emphasis on greatly increased responsibility for lay people in the Church as continuing to grow. In the future, John Garvey writes in an extraordinarily perceptive chapter of *Tomorrow's Church,* "because of the decline in the numbers of priests, lay people will be called on increasingly to serve as ministers of the eucharist, catechists and leaders of prayer in places where there are not enough priests to go around." This, you may say is the conventional wisdom but Garvey goes on to point out that "if baptism is the sacrament which makes us Christians, . . . lay people are not properly seen as amateur Christians, clients of the clergy. Clericalism and anti-clericalism are both on the way out of the church's practice."

It is hard to believe that any development in *Tomorrow's Church* can have more significance than this revivified understanding of the meaning of baptism. "Baptism," Garvey reminds us, "is the sign that we were chosen to be what we are from all eternity, a sign that our choices matter less than God's—infinitely less." And if, increasingly, we come to realize that the identification of all Catholics as joined in baptism is primary, questions of roles for bishops, priests, religious and lay people, of women and minorities ought to diminish in importance and ultimately, with the grace of God, disappear.

Tomorrow's Church is an insightful and challenging treatment of a subject that could not be more important. Its contributors have done their job well, providing us with imaginative and thoughtful treatment of many perplexing questions. It should be helpful to many.

Robert E. Burns
Executive Editor
U.S. Catholic

Chapter One

LAITY

by John Garvey

THE place of the layperson in the church has been an odd one since the earliest centuries of Christian history. In a way which might seem paradoxical it can be compared to the place of the monk. Thomas Merton has helped to popularize the image of the monk as a marginal man, a person whose existence makes little or no sense to the existing political and religious establishments. His job, in a way, is *not* to fit in; it is to stand alone, and in so standing to reveal something essential about what it means to be a Christian.

The monastic movement was originally lay. That is to say, it was made up of people who were not only *not* concerned with being ordained or finding a place in the structure of the church; they even avoided ordination. They did so not because it is a bad thing to be ordained, but for other reasons, which have to do with what it means to be a layperson as well as with what it means to be a monk.

Before making any projections about what the future of the laity might be like it is necessary to pay some attention to past and present attitudes towards lay Catholicism, which means paying some attention

16

as well to what it means to belong to a church which has over-emphasized the clerical state, at least since the time of the reformation and counter-reformation.

Catholic clericalism is not so much a matter of doctrine as it is a habit, a conventional attitude. Rome still speaks of a laicized priest in terms which are condescending, to say the least: such a person has been "reduced" to the lay state. Lay Catholics who are serious about their religion are sometimes asked why they didn't become priests or nuns. The assumption here is that religion is a profession, like law, and priests and nuns are its professionals. Lay people are, presumably, their clients. This clericalism is hardly confined to Catholicism. In most religious organizations there is an equivalent: the congregation hires a professional Christian or a professional Jew, a man or woman who visits the sick, comforts the afflicted, weeps or rejoices with the bereaved or the blessed.

What needs to be examined here is not the belief that the community can benefit from more or less official representatives—this seems to be an organizational necessity—but rather the belief that this representation is something which brings with it the status which we accord to other professionals, to doctors or lawyers, for example. (We ought to examine that status critically, but such an examination isn't the point of this essay.) The future of lay Catholicism will see the collapse of many of these assumptions, which came about for historical and political reasons more than for theological ones. Clerical status became important in a worldly way—that is to say, as a matter of prestige—as the church became an important political entity, one of the several kinds of power which bound an empire together. The worldly, coercive power of the church has been on the wane for years, but we remain used to the idea that there is a two-fold sort of Christianity, composed of people who have chosen to make a profession of being Christian, and those who are Christians by birth or some other, more casual form of association. As the social reasons for being Christian fade, so will the distinction between the clergyman, seen as a professional Christian, and the layman, seen more or less as an accidental or amateur Christian.

Clerical assumptions have gotten in the way of necessary considerations of the role of the Christian in the world, and they have confused the debate over such issues as the ordination of women and married men. (Perhaps we should speak of *clericalist* rather than clerical assumptions, since many clergymen are not saddled with them, and many laypeople are.) Part of the confusion has to do with what the word *vocation* means. Its earliest use was not at all like its current, rather cloudy one. Now a vocation to the priesthood is popularly thought of as something which comes more or less directly from God, a yearning or desire which parents and teachers and friends ought to encourage, to keep it from being entangled and hindered. But "vocation," or "calling," originally meant a call from a particular bishop, who called a person who was (ideally, though this was honored more in theory than in practice) chosen by the community to be their priest. The idea that a vocation to the priesthood comes from God in a way which is somehow different from the simple calling to Christianity is rather late, and has all sorts of attendant problems. For one thing, it has tended to make the priesthood appear to be the superior way of being Christian. Priesthood as a form of high status is a problem, though, given the fact that Christianity calls us to a way of life which stands ordinary notions of status on their heads.

Any discussion of what it means to be a layperson must touch in passing on something which has been said so many times that it is close to becoming a cliché; but it is, unfortunately, necessary to point out that the word *laity* comes from the Greek *laos,* which means "people." The church is the people who make it up, and the offices which occur within the church are there to serve the people. They are not ends in themselves, but exist for a reason Paul describes in Ephesians 4: there are in the church many gifts and "appointments" which exist in order to build up the community, so that we can all "realize our common unity through faith in the Son of God, and fuller knowledge of him. So we shall reach perfect manhood, that maturity which is proportioned to the completed growth of Christ." We are to be measured by what Christ is; we are, Paul says, to grow into him, to become in some sense what he is. This is the calling of the community and of every individual in the community. This is the only purpose for which any sort of office or ministry exists in the church; and the purpose is skewed fatally in the wrong direction whenever ministry of any sort is seen as a form of status or authority which places us above others.

Clericalism must be considered a bit before we talk about what it means to be a member of the laity, partly because it plays a large part in the way laypeople regard themselves. The greatest problem with clericalism is that it makes the church look like a class system in which serious membership is determined by the access of the lowest members to the privileges, status, and functions of those at the top. This attitude has an effect on lay workers within the church, and results in a kind of lay clericalism. In a magazine interview one lay minister who works with religious education programs complained that he should have the same status as a priest saying the Mass. The words he used were terrible: he said that his office should have the same "prestige." Similarly, a man who left the seminary complained that his married status and active church involvement were not recognized and acknowledged the way the activities of priests are. Some form of official church approval plainly mattered to him. A few of the people who have argued for the ordination of women have made the worst possible argument for their arguable cause: they have complained that women are second-class citizens in the church. (Using their argument it can be said that they are wrong by a class. All married men are second-class citizens; women are third class citizens.) The church should have no first class citizens at all, but this doesn't seem to have occurred to people who argue that their place in the church should be accompanied by some form of prestige, status, or officially recognized importance. Any person who desires leadership ought to be distrusted, especially if that person claims to be part of a tradition which exalts the servant and the slave, and contrasts its forms of leadership with those of the world in which the great lord it over others, and "like to be called benefactors" (Luke 22:25). In the world's ordinary way of doing things, those in power "like to make their authority felt" (Mark 10:42), but "that is not to be the way with you." There are, of course, a lot of ways—some of them very subtle—in which authority can be made to be felt.

The problem with church authority is similar to the problem which faces any bureaucracy: it can be forgotten that it exists for a reason other than its own growth and maintenance. It is not an end in itself. Hierarchical authority exists to oversee the handing on of the gospel, and the distribution of the sacraments, and to make sure that this is done in an orthodox manner.

"Orthodoxy" is a word which has come to have some unattractive resonances, but it is a concept which matters. Christianity is about certain essential things which can be distorted, made monstrous, or forgotten. The authority of the church to say that some ideas and directions are destructive has traditionally been located in bishops (although as we will

see it is not necessarily always to be found there).
Without this function the church would lapse either
into elitism or mob rule. Bishops were originally
made bishops by election or acclaim, and even today
they must be approved; the point is that they cannot
be self-ordained. If they are "charismatic" it is an ac-
cident. Their job is to be competent at reading the
tradition and handing it on, and although it is not a
glamorous thing, simple competence isn't bad. There
are more exciting ways of trying to lead people than
the kind which comes from putting orthodoxy and
simple fidelity to the gospel at the center, but they
aren't necessarily good. The alternative to the authority of an uninteresting bishop might really be Jim
Jones.

Orthodoxy has been abused—or rather, people
have used the idea of orthodoxy to defend abusive
behavior—but its basic protective function should
not be obscured: it is the right of people who are
Christians to have a number of people within the
church whose job it is to see whether what is being
claimed as Christian fits in with the whole of Christian tradition. Too often "Christian tradition" has
been equated with the prevailing mood of the ecclesiastical administration, but the importance of the office can't be dismissed because it has been abused.

On the other hand, there is a limit to this vocation.
Bishops help to preserve orthodoxy and ordain
priests to celebrate the sacraments for the larger
community. Beyond that their specific competence,
essential as it is, ends. Bishops and priests finally

find themselves where the rest of us find ourselves: having to see what the gospel says to us, and respond to it. Orthodoxy and the sacraments are not ends in themselves. They exist for a reason. The mystery of Christianity begins at this point, and so does the question of what it means to be a lay Christian.

It is necessary to say these things because a lot of people have a way of identifying the church with its hierarchical structure. (This is particularly true of very conservative Catholics and anti-Catholics, who curiously share a vision of Catholicism as a monolithic and authoritarian thing.) Before the lay vocation and its future can be understood, it must be seen that the church exists for a purpose which transcends its structure. If that purpose is not shown forth by the laity—if that showing-forth is not in fact seen as the vocation of the laity—then the structure of the church and all considerations of church authority are beside the point.

While the special province of the ordained clergy is the ordinary administration of the sacraments and the deliverance of orthodox teaching, the way in which the sacraments are administered, and the orthodoxy of the teaching, must be open to the insight of the people who are to hear, act, teach, and themselves bear fruit. This idea—that the "non-official" church is also the teaching church, to which the church as a whole must listen—is shrugged off by some conservatives as a recent liberal notion, but in fact the decisions of church councils have been rejected by the body of the faithful in ways which stuck: we do not believe a lot of things which were solemnly declared by councils. We should thank God for that fact, given the unfortunate reality that some of this officially sanctioned teaching included endorsements of anti-Semitism and encouragements to make holy wars. But the function of the lay office here, the final acceptance or rejection of bad hierarchical ideas, is not merely a negative one. It involves more than ignoring bad ideas; or rather, ignoring bad ideas can perform a positive doctrinal function. Cardinal Newman pointed out that it was the laity and the monks, not the hierarchy "in charge," who resisted the Arian heresy. They resisted against the inclination of the pope and imperially inclined bishops, who wanted a compromise. Even the limitation of sacramental celebration to the clergy is not all that constant. There is a passage in Tertullian which implies that any Christian might be expected to act as a minister of the sacraments, and at various points in church history abbots have ordained monks to celebrate the eucharist without waiting for bishops to do the job right, and laypeople have heard confessions.

I don't wish to recommend a wild and woolly approach to church administration, but only to suggest that a lot of Catholic history proves that orthodoxy and sacrament are not hierarchical franchises.

The limits of what look like Catholic "assignments" become clear during times of profound cultural change. Just as Christianity became legal and relatively safe, the monastic movement began. It

looked wild and unclerical to some, but it turned out
to be a source of creative energy for the church during the dark ages, a time which saw the collapse of
some forms of authority and the rise of new forms. It
could be that our time is simply a confusing period
which will give away in some simple fashion to a
new and less confusing time; but that isn't really
likely.

People entering and leaving the ages which we
now describe as "dark" didn't think of themselves as
people who were moving in and out of periods which
would have clear historical labels, nor did people at
the start of the Reformation. But they did know themselves to be going through a time of questioning, a
shake-up time. It will take some distance to see what
our own period means, but the shake-up is clear
enough. Clergymen, monks, nuns, and laypeople
wonder why they are what they are, and look for the
deep sense—for the meaning which must be the basis
of our choice. And if that choice is not a clear one,
why continue with it?

Some problems can be found with this desire to
have everything clear and simple, but the demand for
clarity can help in redefinition. Some problems with
the old forms become clear. Some problems with
new assumptions also become clear when people
whose background has been formed by a rich tradition like Catholicism strain forward from a past
whose cultural references have collapsed towards an
unknown future. They believe that the tradition matters deeply, even if some of its past uses and inter-

pretations are not now helpful. We still believe that those dormant references may make some sense at some other time; we are not willing simply to abandon them as if the judgment of the contemporary world were final. At the same time, we cannot accept the assumptions of the past as unchallengeable, or think in terms of Christendom—of a time when power and official Christianity were comfortable bedfellows. Perhaps the collapse of Christendom has its echo in the insistence on the priesthood of all the faithful. Just as an officially sanctioned form of Christianity is not protected and encouraged by the state, so within the church itself the meaning of hierarchy and ministry is changing. What it means to be lay or clerical is coming to be seen as a secondary question, secondary to the more basic question: what does it mean to be a Christian of any sort? The answer to this question is the key to the future not only of lay Catholicism, but of Christianity.

A couple of cases have brought this to the fore, in different ways. One is the case of Father Drinan, who was asked (*asked* is a polite word here) to resign his congressional office because the Vatican has said that priests should not be involved directly in politics. The other is the case of those priests who are involved in running the government of Nicaragua.

Politics is, I agree, a dirty business. Politicians are asked to do all sorts of things which ordinarily decent people wouldn't dream of doing. But my question is this: why are such activities considered all right for lay people? The Vatican has done nothing to prevent priests from becoming professors, artists, or administrators. Is there something inherently evil about politics? As someone whose tendencies are towards Christian anarchism, I think there is. But if there is it should affect lay people as much as it does the clergy.

The idea that priests have a special place as representatives of Catholicism makes sense, from one point of view: they are the public presiders over Catholic functions, and are known to represent the Catholic community in a way which very few lay people do. But because each Catholic also represents Catholicism and ought to feel responsible for it, the belief that it is somehow wrong for Fr. Drinan to hold public office, but all right for Eugene McCarthy, implies several wrong things at once. One is that lay people are not held to the same Christian standards as priests. Another is that lay people are allowed to do slightly scandalous things, while priests are either too good (or, worse, ought to be seen as being too good) for that sort of thing. Another is that those anti-Catholics who worry about Catholics in public office are quite right: Fr. Drinan resigned an office to which he was elected by his fellow citizens on orders from Rome. That is what anti-Catholic Americans always said was wrong with Catholicism, and it happened in this case. The Vatican controlled the activity of one of its own. The argument that the priesthood cannot allow an allegiance divided between the demands of politics and the duties of the priesthood raises a couple of questions: given the fact that the priesthood equips a person only for the administration of the sacraments, is the ordained Christian to do nothing but administer the sacraments? If he does do something else, why is it all right to be a university administrator (a form of work which can be vicious, as can journalistic status-seeking, or, for that matter, the running of a parish) but not an elected representative? Why is this activity acceptable for lay people who have been baptized into the death and resurrection of Christ, and not for those who have been ordained? Is baptism a lesser mystery?

And this brings us to what it means to be a lay person, and what it will mean, because the primary sacrament is baptism. Even the eucharist is in an important sense an emphasis or shining forth of what baptism means. Baptism calls us into the life which God shares with us, the life revealed in Jesus' death and resurrection. Baptism is our participation in that death and rising, and our lives are attempts to realize, through falling and rising—and finally dying and rising—the depths of what we received, and continue to receive, because of baptism.

Any consideration of what it means to be a lay person—which is to say, what it means simply to be a Christian—must begin with the meaning of baptism. Perhaps because baptism happened to most of us as infants we do not take it as seriously as we should. We continue to receive the eucharist, and it properly occupies a central place in Catholic self-understanding. We were married or ordained or took religious vows as adults (at least we thought of ourselves as

adults at the time, though later reflection may lead us
to qualify that perception) and these events loom
large in our self-understanding. But baptism is the
great mystery. It is the sign that we were chosen to be
what we are from all eternity, a sign that our choices
matter less than God's—infinitely less. John's first letter tells us: "In this is love, not that we loved God but
that he loved us and sent his Son to be the expiation
for our sins;" and "we love, because he first loved
us." Baptism brings us up against this reality as no
other sacrament does. While there are good arguments to be made against the practice of infant baptism, a good argument for it could be that there is no
better symbol of our true state than the helplessness
of a baby before the love of God. Our personal conversion matters less to God, though it must come
over the long haul, than his choice of us. In this context it is interesting that the church has taught from
ancient times that baptism can be administered by
lay people, as if to say, that when it gets down to
basics—when it gets down to the absolute center of
the faith—the clerical structure matters less than the
urgency which is the point of Christianity: we are
called to share, through baptism, through this gift
which is God's calling to us, in the life of God revealed in Christ.

If baptism is the sacrament which makes us Christians, and if the other sacraments are in a way de-
clensions from this central thing which has happened in our lives, what does it mean?

Among other things, it certainly means that lay

people are not properly seen as amateur Christians, clients of the clergy. Clericalism and anti-clericalism are both on their way out of the church's practice, partly for reasons of pastoral necessity. Because of the decline in the numbers of priests, lay people will be called on increasingly to serve as ministers of the eucharist, catechists, and leaders of prayer in places where there are not enough priests to go around. The current situation is not entirely satisfactory. It is better to have a Mass than a prayer service at which communion is distributed; the latter is not as clearly a memorial of the Last Supper as is the Mass, which puts the eucharist in its proper context. But this is likely to be the continuing pattern in a church which is experiencing both a declining number of priests, and a leadership which is unwilling to allow the ordination of married men or of women.

Necessity will force a redefinition of the distinctions which have traditionally been made between clergy and laity. The principle of necessity in Catholic change has been an important one, and its virtue was made clear to me by a missionary priest who answered a nun's objection to a change in church policy, one which she thought should have been made years before because it was "the right thing to do." "I don't agree," he said, "because when you change on principle you build the damn principle into your system and you can't get rid of it. It's much wiser to change only when you have to." If the ministry of lay people is recognized out of necessity (and here we should remember that the ministry of lay people was considered a very uncatholic idea not too long ago) that isn't necessarily a bad thing, especially where ministry has been seen as a form of status or community approval. Ministry cannot be created by fiat from above, but ought to spring from the real needs of a particular community.

The question of "the place of the laity" is, however, a much more profound one than whether or not the laity can "be entrusted" with ministries which were formerly restricted to priests.

For reasons we cannot fathom we are called to be Christians, a vocation which happened "from before the beginning of time." As lay people we have no status in this, no career to make, nothing that can profit us. To seek official church recognition would confuse this status, which is important precisely because it is empty. The calls by some lay people for official church recognition seem to me to be ill-advised. Francis of Assisi may have been ordained to the diaconate, but we know that he was not a priest. He could also not be accused of anticlericalism. His insistence on respect for the priesthood was more than most priests could stomach without blushing. But when some of his first brothers in the order wanted to have episcopal permission to preach guaranteed, Francis objected. "Let it be your unique privilege," he said, "to have no privilege."

This may help towards an understanding of what the lay vocation must begin to be. Francis' statement is a sign of what the church, now more than ever before, must look towards. To lack privilege is to lack

an important form of power, but that very weakness
is not necessarily bad; it is in fact necessary in gospel
terms. The loss of clerical privilege, the loss of temporal power, are seen by that odd alliance of conservative Catholics and anti-Christians in exactly the
same way: this spells the doom of Christianity, both
agree. And if Christianity could be equated with the
worldly power of the church they would certainly be
right. When there was such a thing as Christendom,
to be a lay Christian was simply to be a citizen. Until
rather recently people tended to belong to a church
because it was the respectable thing to do, or because
of a kind of inertia: my parents were Catholic, therefore I am a Catholic. But as many Catholic parents
have found out, this no longer applies. There are no
socially compelling reasons to be Christian now. It is
a matter of choice, one influenced by background to
be sure; but the reasons to be Christian are no longer
compelling. To be Christian now is more a free decision than it has been since the Edict of Milan.

So what does all this mean for the future of the
laity? Several things. There will probably continue to
be a decline in the number of churchgoing Catholics,
although for reasons of background people may still
identify themselves as Catholic, without bothering to
do much about it. Barring a change in the Vatican's
insistence on clerical celibacy, there will continue to
be a shortage of priests, and lay Catholics will have
to take over several of the duties which were reserved to priests in the past. This has already begun
to happen, in the use of lay ministers for the dis-

tribution of communion, the use of lay catechists, and in places where there is a shortage of priests the use of lay leaders in conducting Sunday worship services. All of this has been pointed out before.

There is, however, another aspect of the church's future which hasn't had enough attention paid to it. The version of church authority which most Christians have been used to (ever since Constantine made Christianity the state religion) was based upon an alliance between the authority of the emperor or king or state, and the leaders of the church. The secularism which began to affect society with the Renaissance and Enlightenment eroded the basis of that alliance. The churches are tolerated or ignored by the state. The church can offer its services to the state as a kind of bribe to insure its survival, like the version of Russian Orthodoxy which is currently tolerated in the Soviet Union. The Moral Majority aims at a church which will serve America the same way, but they do this voluntarily, in the grip of a more vicious delusion: apparently they accept America as the Fifth Gospel. Some liberation theologians would have the church serve revolutionary regimes the way the Moral Majority wants the church to serve Amerca. I have the strong feeling that all of these phenomena are the last gasps of the sort of Christianity which was certified by Constantine, the Christianity which must be on what the world considers the winning side.

But liberation theology has also given signs of the future church. The "base communities" of the Latin

American church recognize and make use of lay initiative. In this they are surprisingly like charismatic renewal groups in other parts of the world. Both the base communities and the charismatic movement have, in different but very important ways, started to dismantle old notions of a compartmentalized Christian life. This acceptance of the idea that life can be divided—that one's religious life is different from one's business or academic or sexual life—was another of Constantine's legacies. It was never a matter of church doctrine, of course, but it was commonly accepted that the Christian life consisted of ethical behavior, churchgoing, and a rather uncritical assent to the decisions of secular and religious authorities. It was not commonly understood that Christianity is about a real and thorough transformation of individuals and societies. The compartmentalized life had its analog in the division between lay and clerical states, a division which is also beginning to crumble. The end of a belief in the compartmentalized life will have far-reaching consequences. People committed to the pro-life cause, and people committed to an end to the arms race, have recognized the fact that there are moral issues with social consequences, and they are acting on their beliefs. The world of public behavior and the world of true devotion are not easily separated.

Another side of this will be an increase in factionalism. A Jewish friend of mine, who is as irritated with his synagogue as many Catholic friends are

with their churches, once said to me, "Soon the only
people who will bother to go to church will be the
people who care deeply about the tradition, and the
fanatics." (The problem is that the fanatics will think
they belong to the first group.) His point was that
people who used to be religiously observant for social reasons will have dropped out, and the people
who are left will either endure one another, or be at
one another's throats. The church in Holland bears
this out, with its severe split between progressives
and conservatives; there are churches in Latin America which have split along similar lines for political
reasons. To a lesser degree there are American parishes which have been pressed to move in one direction or another, in a way foreign to Catholics of the
past.

Because Catholics today feel free to reject aspects
of the church's moral teaching which in the past
would have been seen as part of a seamless garment,
to be accepted or rejected as a whole, this factionalism can be expected to continue. It isn't a good thing,
but it is perhaps an inevitable result of the Roman
tendency to over-define. To insist on too much is to
create a brittle structure. To be authoritative beyond
one's real competence is to undermine one's real authority.

But at the center of the storm, the Catholic emphasis on the reality of God's presence in the world, the
belief that this presence is as real and basic as bread,
wine, water, love-making—the "matter of sacra-

ments"—will still be at the center of the church, and prayer will still turn us towards the depths which the sacraments indicate.

The influence of the church as an institution among other institutions (the press, the government, the university) will probably continue to decline. But perhaps that influence was not the sort of influence Christianity was meant to have. When social rewards, respectability, and community acceptance are entwined with Christianity something of the gospel's essential message is obscured. This may not be the end of Christianity, but rather the beginning of a new form of Christianity, one which will travel light where privilege and power are concerned. Priesthood has lost its status. Being a layperson never had any. Now the question is more pointed than ever before: Why does it make sense for you to be what you are? That question will either be answered in the lives of laypeople or it will not be answered at all.

The danger here is a new form of churchiness. Baron von Hugel, the great Catholic lay theologian, wrote to his Anglican niece that it was important not to confuse churchiness with true religion. As necessity dictates, more Catholics will be involved in ministries which were formerly reserved to priests, and much of the ordinary administration of the church will be turned over to laypeople.

But if this trend reinforces the clerical model of the church by creating a new kind of lay cleric it will not do what badly needs doing: it will not offer an answer to the question, "Why are you a Christian?"

If our lives are in every respect like the lives of the people who do not believe that life has any meaning at all, we can be accused of holding on to our belief simply because it consoles us. (On the other hand, we should not change our lives simply to prove them wrong. The way we live should reflect real conviction, or we should be honest enough to admit our own practical atheism. But even here, in our confusion, we have to be careful to avoid the reduction of Christianity to a particular set of ethics. We are always being led on, and the greatest danger is to think we have arrived, at last, at being truly Christian.)

In any case, the great task of Christians is to make clear in their lives the truth of what they profess to believe. That can only be done through prayer and an attentive listening to the gospel. This has always been the task of the Christian, but it is revealed in its clarity in a time which has little respect for institutional Christianity. This is where lay people have a clear and definite ministry. A lot of non-believers expect priests and ministers to try to sell them on religion, just as all of us expect insurance salesmen to sell us on insurance. The fact that the lay person has nothing to gain is the advantage of the lay person. If it makes sense to choose Catholic Christianity (or "mere Christianity," as C. S. Lewis would put it, or belief in anything over nihilism) it could be that the person with nothing to gain from his belief is the best person to present the case for belief.

This, however, looks like a plea for a too-deliberate approach to convert-making. We are told that we should be "the salt of the earth," the thing which all by itself makes what the world is worth keeping (because salt is not only a seasoning but also a preservative). We are asked, in a time which has little respect for the idea that our yearning for meaning, for truth, is built into the universe, to be people who exhibit that search and that finding in our own lives. The challenge is more pointed than it ever was, and this is our hope.

There is the hope, then, that necessity will move the church into new and important areas of self-understanding. But there is a counter-trend. I am afraid that the current form of American religion will allow the churches to offer their dwindling congregations the reassurance that there is nothing basically wrong with their assumptions about life. I know it is a gloomy thing to say, but failure to confront the murderous nature of our time, something which involves bombs, power, domination, abortion, and wealth, all of them entwined—this is the great sin of church. The laity are as entangled as the hierarchy in all of this, and to wait for the hierarchy to lead the rest of the church out of the mess is a mistake. The way out can be found only by taking a deep breath, and beginning to act as Christians who do not need to wait for leaders to act, but who need instead to see what the gospel tells them.

Chapter Two

PARISH

Thomas A. Kleissler

"My parish small group made me an 'out of
the closest Catholic.' What do I mean by
that? For the first time in my life I can now
share my faith with other people. For the
first time, I feel comfortable in talking about
Jesus to my own children. Sounds like a terrible thing to say, but I bet lots of Catholics
like me have a problem talking about the
Lord even with those they love most."

THIS is how one member of a northern New Jersey
parish expressed his new sense of joy and freedom in
being able to share what was really important to him
although it had too long been tucked away deeply in
the recesses of his heart.

"O God our hearts were made for you and they
shall not rest until they rest in you." With great wisdom, St. Augustine, many centuries ago, expressed
the deep longing of the human heart for the ultimate
love, God.

But, today, in a world whose activity and expansion is so rapid that the earth itself seems to spin ever
faster on its axis, where and how are we to experi-

ence our God? While hermitages offer opportunity
for a contemplative relationship with God, the hope
for most people is in their parish life. The parish
therefore is a key factor if the Church is to have any
significant influence on the average person.

As the U.S. Catholic bishops have said, "The parish is for most Catholics the single most important
part of the church. This is where for them the mission of Christ continues. This is where they publicly
express their faith, joining with others to give proof
of their communion with God and with one another."[1] The statement goes on to say parish must
be concerned with "developing the structure necessary for supporting its community life and carrying
out its mission."

The responsibility of mission was clearly proclaimed to the apostles by Jesus after his resurrection: "Peace be to you! As the Father has sent me so I
am sending you." This sense of mission was further
amplified in 1 John 1:3, "What we have seen and
heard we are telling you so that you too may be in
union with us, as we are in union with the Father
and with his Son Jesus Christ."

Jesus has come to give life to all people, to bring us
into unity with the triune God and to reach out and
restore all things to God. As the basic component of
church, the parish has primary responsibility for this
mission both today and tomorrow.

Thus, the basic question is *how* will the parish of
the future provide people with the opportunity to
participate fully in this mission and enable them to

develop a strong personal relationship with God? I believe the answer is already evolving. My optimism is based on my extensive parish experience, along with a broad view of parish life in many areas of the United States seen as director of the Office of Pastoral Renewal in the Archdiocese of Newark. This long association "in the field" has led me to a firm conviction that the best pastoral approach towards aiding people in developing a deeper relationship with God is through involvement in small Christian communities. I have witnessed how such communal relationships have enabled and empowered fulfillment of Christ's mission. It is for this reason that I believe the trend toward basic communities will continue to expand and will have great impact on parish life in the future.

Today, literally thousands of parish small groups are beginning to develop the strong personal relationship with Jesus that is required to build the sort of dynamic leadership essential for the realization of Christian goals and ideals. In the small group setting, men, women and youth, virtual "strangers" to the mission bestowed upon them at their baptism, are experiencing the warm embrace of the Father and the transforming power of the Holy Spirit. Among friends and peers they are finding it comfortable to discuss their spiritual experiences. As a result, their prayer life is strengthened, interest in scripture is advanced, a Christ-centered social conscience is being developed and subsequent Christian actions are often becoming a new way of life.

These small groups, numbering 15 or less people, allow for the building of good personal relationships that foster open intellectual and spiritual growth based on Catholic teaching. A community is truly formed when, in addition to the sharing of life and faith experiences and the focusing on prayer and scripture, the group moves beyond support for each member and develops an outward direction that leads them to be of service to the larger parish and the world beyond.

Surveys have indicated that average parish participation beyond Sunday Mass today involves only 12 percent of the people. Parishes actively promoting small communities, however, can easily double or triple that percentage. And I am convinced that those figures will continue to rise in the future.

Basic Christian communities have been in existence for some time, both in concept and in practice. In the past, however, although they have provided powerful formation for most who have belonged to them, they often were viewed with suspicion and charged with elitism and divisiveness. In his apostolic exhortation "On Evangelism in the Modern World," Pope Paul VI called attention to "these 'small communities' or *communautés de base,* because they are often talked about in the Church today." In noting that they should be the special beneficiaries of evangelization and at the same time evangelizers themselves, he emphasized that *ecclesial* communautés de base, "those [groups] which come together within the Church in order to unite them-

selves to the Church and to cause the Church to grow
. . . will be a hope for the universal church." These
groups, he said, "spring from the need to live the
church's life more intensely, or from the desire and
quest for a more human dimension such as larger ecclesial communities can only offer with difficulty, especially in the big modern cities which lend themselves both to life in the mass and to anonymity."

Presently, many thousands of small groups are
flourishing because of the encouragement and pastoral leadership of bishops and pastors and in some
cases they are developing at such a rapid rate that
they are becoming accepted as a regular part of
parish life.

I can remember, 25 years ago, when I was studying
for the priesthood, that those who became involved
in small groups were a rare exception. The Young
Christian Workers and Students and the couples in
the Christian Family Movement were seen as "rad-
icals" who "threatened the Church." These organizations, with their small group philosophy were considered to be a "fringe" element in the Church.

A few years later, after my ordination, we were
able to enroll some 400 people in small CCD discussion groups in my parish. Even that kind of small
group involvement, as non-threatening as it was, was
unusual.

My own interest in small groups began, I think, as
far back as the fifth grade, when Sister Catherine
Patricia talked about the "missions." Her understanding of the role of all the people of God sparked

in me a sensitivity to my own mission in the church. Later, as a freshman in high school, it occurred to me that the degree of success in any venture depended on the full effort of all. I noticed, for instance, that workers in factories had more impact on productivity than did the owners. At the same time, I became aware of how much the lay people in our parish relied on the priests and religious to do the "church's" work. It became apparent that if the Church were truly going to influence the world, all the people had to get involved, particularly since there were some areas only the laity could reach.

Still later, I came upon a Young Christian Worker pamphlet that made sense to me because its members remained very much in the world and were dealing with real life issues. I enthusiastically accepted the Cardijn process and it became a part of my life. It was in 1956, however, at a combined CFM and YCW convention at Notre Dame, that I was exposed to the quiet fire of Monsignor Hillenbrand. He, at last, released in me my energy for the development of small communities.

My 19 years of parish experience, both in urban and suburban areas, proved the value of the small group dynamic. I have witnessed transformations in a multitude of men, women and youth who have been exposed to the observe, judge and act methodology of CFM, YCS and other special formation programs. I have seen lay leadership develop and direct the movement toward shared responsibility via parish and pastoral councils, as well as ministerial programs in liturgy, education, and pastoral and social service.

As director of Pastoral Renewal, this experience was intrinsic to the development of RENEW, a three-year diocesan wide spiritual renewal effort highlighting the small group concept which has spread to a good number of dioceses across the nation. Bishop Eugene J. Gerber of the Diocese of Dodge City says of the process: "We need to begin in small groups with the realization that every individual action has a cumulative effect on others. We can take a lesson from the American Indian who builds a small fire and moves closer to it to get warm. The White Man builds a large fire and stands back. RENEW has as one of its strengths the building of small fires that will help to transform personal and collective consciences of people, as well as the activities in which they engage, their lives and concrete surroundings. This is the way Christ began. This is evangelization."

In the Archdiocese of Newark, some 40,000 participated in RENEW small groups and through this process it is now not uncommon to see many parishes choosing to remain involved in small group sharing.

It is not merely the numbers of people in small groups that is satisfying. Even more significant is the spiritual impact that comes from the small groups on the lives of the people involved and how the process has motivated them to reach out in service to others.

During the course of my priesthood, it has become very clear to me that there are increasing numbers who wish to be nourished through involvement in small communities. No longer considered to be underground or "kooky," parish small communities have moved into the mainstream of parish life.

The power of the small group dynamic may be more clearly illustrated in the following case histories:

In St. Joseph's Parish, Oradell, New Jersey, after only a month and a half of scripture discussion in small groups, a course was offered so that the people might receive a deeper understanding of the meaning of the written Word. The study session was offered at 1:30 Tuesday afternoon—hardly a prime-time. Twenty-five chairs were set up to accommodate the expected participants. To the delight and surprise of the organizers, 150 people turned up, including some who temporarily closed their businesses in order to participate.

At St. Anthony's in Elizabeth, small group involvement and scripture sharing was so meaningful and striking that participants did not want to take the scheduled two-month break when the Thanksgiving holiday arrived. They asked to continue to meet weekly through the Christmas season to learn more about the scriptures and pray together. Many of the participants, whose first language was Italian, wanted to know where they could obtain Italian bibles.

"Leave those concerns to Jane Fonda" was the reaction of Sal DePasquale, a small group leader in Holy Family Parish in Nutley, New Jersey, when he was introduced to RENEW material calling for involvement in the world's problems. "We don't need this! We're honest working people, raising our children and doing a good job. Why do we have to be worrying about all these other problems?" These were the candid reactions of Sal and some of his fellow group members at the start of the RENEW semester on social concerns. But yet, just a few weeks—and much painful soul searching—later, Sal and his group agreed that this series of meetings was even more satisfying and productive than earlier semesters. They have taken a keen interest in the problem of starvation in Cambodia. A jar filled with money sits on the table around which they gather to meet. The cash—earmarked to support a starving child—represents savings from fasting and reduction in personal expenses. The object is to give not only from their abundance, but rather to the point of sacrifice. Sal has concluded that the whole experience has been extremely gratifying. "It's made me more mature," he says, "Now I understand that the problems of the world can be affected by my personal relationship with Jesus and that ordinary people can make a difference."

The fact is that small groups provoke a more personal awareness and understanding of our Christian mission. As Ralph Keifer put it in his article "Christian Initiation: The State of the Question," the (church's) focus on institutions rather than persons has resulted in a dependence upon culture to sustain Christian life and Christian identity.[2] He warns that this is dangerous because the values of our culture, which is perceived to be fundamentally Christian, are ambiguous and may be eroding those institutions. He further claims that "the retention of a pattern appropriate to the established church implies the retention of pastoral patterns which presume rather than attempt to evoke its radical conversion."

Our goal then should be to develop a structure that will enable the parish to become a living, Christian community. This means we have to start by forming strong leadership—people who have undergone solid personal growth and experience continuing spiritual renewal. I believe that such leadership will emerge from small groups because, properly developed, they become truly Christian communities with all the implications of that status.

Father Blaine G. Barr, pastor of the parish community of St. Joseph, New Hope, Minnesota, defines such a Christian community in its fullest capacity as "a sacrament, the place where people meet the Lord and encounter his saving word and action. It is a group of people who express an explicit faith that Jesus is Lord, ratify this faith through rites of Christian initiation, deepen this faith by growing to know and love Christ better through the Gospels, seal this faith in the Eucharist and witness this faith by finding ways to serve Christ in others through practiced application of the Christian message to their daily lives."[3]

I believe that such communities are not only formed by, but also help form, strong leaders. Indeed, the stimulus of shared, solid spiritual experiences and sincere dedicated people provoke exciting ideas that are the catalyst for dynamic Christian leadership.

Some 15 years ago, I was certain that the parish I was assigned to as a "second curate," was prepared to institute a good number of more permanent small communities. Between 25 and 50 leaders—products of small group development—were willing and eager to assume increased pastoral responsibility. Their obvious competence, strong personalities and enthusiasm would have facilitated the building of communities around them and the parish would have been greatly strengthened by this development. Unfortunately, the time was not quite ripe for such an undertaking to be accepted as a part of mainstream parish life.

It was at that time the vision of the *parish as a community of communities* started to become clear. Today, there are many parishes ready to give such an idea serious consideration. The time has come for us to put pastoral considerations first, to allow real leadership to develop and to take the steps that will best enable the parish to flourish.

I am convinced that as the development of basic small communities continues, most parishes as we know them today will begin functioning as "dioceses." The pastor, in effect, will be the "Ordinary," convening the leaders of the small communities on a regular basis. Communities of people will meet in their homes and other places that lend to greater intimacy, sharing and support. The parish church will become a "cathedral," where the communities will meet on a regular basis for common worship. It will also serve as the place of worship for people in the larger community who choose not to belong to small groups.

While such new "dioceses" are doubtless still decades away and will require restructuring of some parishes to accommodate differences in size and resources, a gradual evolution in parish life must begin now so that innovations can be tested each step of the way. More important than adopting any single vision of the future should be our willingness to see the indicators of how the Holy Spirit is working. We have to remain open to the direction the Spirit provides and move along that path. Taking each step in trust is the sign of a faithful people.

We should acknowledge, for instance, several other developments that are taking place both within and outside of small communities. In each instance, however, I believe the basic small communities concept can be integrated into these developments and would even serve to enhance their progress.

These developments include trends toward:

• Personal relationship with Jesus. People will participate in parish life if they have developed a personal relationship with—and a commitment to—Jesus.

• The scriptures as a guiding norm of life. Hunger for God and the search for authentic Christian life will lead to increased study of scripture. The scriptures will be a powerful source of strength for large numbers of people.

• Ministerial development. Both our theology of Church and diminished numbers of priests will continue to encourage the recognition, development and expression of varied forms of lay ministry.

• Shared responsibility. Hand in hand with ministerial development will be an increasing clarification of roles in the parish and an improved understanding of ministerial relationships, including accountability to the community.

• The Adult Catechumenate. The restored rite of initiation will be both a means of introducing people to the faith and also a formation process for ongoing parish activity. The catechumenate, centered on a communal model rather than clerically dominated, will enjoy great success particularly among people who have traditionally rejected the Church's invitation.

• Holistic spirituality. Advances can be expected in prayer life and spiritual contemplation, which will lead to a strong influence on the daily roles people play in society.

• Worship as celebration. Church renovations and full-time liturgical ministers will greatly assist people to experience liturgy as celebration. Careful liturgical planning and preparation will become normative.

• Improved sacramental life. The sacraments will have greater meaning to people rather than being mere ritualistic or cultural "landmarks." Family centered sacramental preparation and reception will be in even greater evidence and healing teams and the Anointing of the Sick will be commonly accepted and in demand.

• The development of organizational and leadership skills. Solid growth calls for more than an expression of good will. Leaders will be required to develop special skills and organizational know-how if rising expectations are to be fulfilled.

• Increased planning. Experience of richer church life will help convince parishioners of the need for planning, goal setting, priorities and ongoing evaluation.

As noted previously, basic Christian communities should have a great influence on these trends. For example, unless the Adult Catechumenate is closely linked with small communities it will be little more than a rehash of conversion classes of the past. For the parish priest to be the organizer and instructor can make the catechumenate merely an updated version of "Fr. Smith Instructs Jackson." At the heart of the catechumenate must be a core community of people thoroughly capable and versed in the catechumenate who are fully qualified to carry out their priestly ministry as the people of God. They need to experience true community themselves if they are to invite others into community. As Keifer has said: It is indeed an incongruity to welcome people into a "community of strangers." Auxiliary small communities would be useful in introducing people to the progressive stages of Pre-catechumenate, Cathechumenate, Enlightenment, Mystagogia. In the final analysis, the catechumenate is a responsibility of the parish community, not just of the individual ordained priest.

Ministerial growth provides another example for small group involvement. If we believe that every baptized Christian is called to ministry, how are these people to discern their ministries? Discovery of the individual's place in the ministerial life of the church happens best and most clearly in small groups. People come to know each other, point up strengths and talents, and affirm each other in directing these personal gifts into ministry. And it is the small group that will support the individual in ministry.

Consider the parish priest who is fortunate enough to have parishioners serve as official parish visitors to the local hospitals on a given day of the week. He may even bring them together once a year for a review of their duties and to strengthen their motivation. Under the small group concept, however, the hospital visitors would come together frequently in community to minister to and encourage one another. Given this continuing support, I believe they would be better prepared to minister to their hospital patients.

Liturgy is another area that can benefit from small community interaction. Although many liturgy committees have been established and their function is now "in vogue," too often they do not realize their real potential for service. Producing good liturgy is presented as the goal, but precious little time is given for the committee to share faith and scripture insights among themselves. How can we expect them to produce good liturgy for the large parish congregation when they themselves have not had the opportunity to experience community?

The small group dynamic, I believe, would also serve to respond to the question, who ministers to the ministers? For me, the answer is an obvious one: ministers should minister to one another. First, ministers should come together in small communities centered on whatever their specialty or service—liturgy, education, etc.—where their particular needs can be recognized, discussed and resolved. From that point, the external expression of their individual ministries could be extended more effectively.

Priests and parish staff persons must find new approaches to fulfill their special calling. Traditional expectations of parishioners of their priests and new demands to develop lay ministries add up to a seemingly impossible task and are forcing changes in the old way of relating to parishioners almost exclusively on a one to one basis. With the prospect of fewer clergy, no priest wants to believe that after years of parish service the future is now bleak. Encouragement and optimism can be drawn, however, from a vision that would permit priests and other staff members to concentrate on the more manageable task of the growth and development of, say, 50 community leaders who in turn influence 500 ministers. We can be sure that the Holy Spirit will not fail us.

The small community approach, it is to be hoped, will put an end to parish committees whose only purpose is productivity or activity for activity's sake. Let us hail the advent of parish communities whose very *life* is the product of their efforts. In truth, such communities will be far more productive in that they strengthen people to the point of real impact and interaction with the world, rather than dealing with the purely parochial concerns that usually take up the vast majority of parish time.

The dynamic of basic Christian Communities motivates people in a new and powerful way. Secular society has left people feeling quite isolated in their faith. Their values and moral standards have been questioned so often that in a subtle but real way they cannot help but wonder what in fact is the truth. The result is a crisis of faith—the greatest problem facing the church of America today.

In the small community, however, doubts, fears and anxieties about basic issues are soon dispelled.

Even the most reluctant joiner usually finds that a trust level develops as concerns about family life, the raising of children and work ethics start to be verbalized. The fact that others can identify with and completely appreciate one's experiences leads to a strengthening of Christian values. In such a situation, the faith experiences of other people can have an impact on a person such as no homily ever has. God becomes more alive to people as they recognize the validity of their faith experiences and hear others share the deep meaning that Jesus has to them and/or their confidence in their loving Father.

What other benefits might this parish direction bring? To name just a few, advancements could be expected in the areas of justice, adult education and evangelization.

Justice now usually represents the weakest area in living out the gospel in a parish. Small communities that are based on prayer, scripture and mutual support have been and will be much better prepared to move into a consideration of justice and its implications in their daily lives. Proceeding at its own pace, the community will ultimately discover its own sense of responsibility for the world around it. Personal experiences such as Sal DePasquale's have moved literally thousands of previously uninvolved parishioners and this phenomenon offers great hope for social justice in the future.

Any conscientious effort directed toward evangelization must raise two serious questions. First, what formation is to be provided for those who are sharing the good news? Secondly, what are we inviting people to? More and more we have to recognize that we can effectively share only from the quality of our own individual experience. Moreover, we cannot expect people to rush to return to what they previously turned away from. To be attractive then, parish life must be renewed. Small communities will provide the formation evangelizers need and also the warm and hospitable atmosphere that will make people feel they are welcomed home. Again experience shows that many people find it more attractive and comfortable to participate in an informal living room discussion among peers than to make a serious inquiry at the church building or rectory.

These considerations lead to fundamental questions about the very nature and structure of parish life. Using Father Dulles' models of church, we know that parish life revolves around the institutional and communal structures. The sacramental, herald and servant models are built upon these structures. In present practice, parish life is heavily weighted toward the institutional structure.

While the institutional model has great strengths in its order and efficiency, it tends however to position people in a listening model, as passive members of the parish. The communal model stresses the church as a more active people and tries to highlight the various roles of people and their relationship one to another. Among its weaknesses is that not enough parishioners have experienced real community.

Thus, it is not a matter of doing away with one

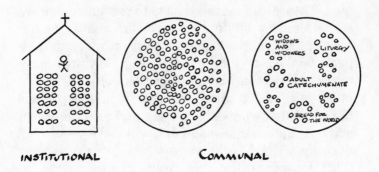

INSTITUTIONAL   COMMUNAL

model or another, but rather to seek a better balance between the two structures. Let the Spirit working in people be the test of where future vitality is to be found. Very likely the future will shift strongly in the direction of a more communal parish.

The word community is not to be used as a magic catch word. As we see from the illustration, when we merely say the "church is people" and lump them together in no particular order, little is gained. We remain large and therefore very likely impersonal. But when people are brought together in smaller groupings they have a chance for a real experience of community.

Worship and sacramental life will primarily be celebrated in the parish church during the earlier stages of the parish's evolution towards a more communal style. In time there may well be a shift toward more frequent celebration of the liturgy and sacramental life within the small communities. Even with these developments there will always be provision in institutional parish life for the parishioner who neither wishes to be, or because of circumstances cannot be, a small community member.

In the meantime, small group members need to be encouraged to participate in other parish activities, reaching out to other parishioners and not simply clustering with small community friends on Sunday morning. The danger of elitism will be greatly reduced by making the small communities a regular part of parish life open to all. The mobility of our society may make some communities short lived, but being part of a small community will not be without benefit, since the concept will be followed in most parishes to which a person may move.

The shift of emphasis and direction in the parish will be gradual in many ways. Existing parish committees will take on a more communal style. Extended periods of prayer and faith-sharing will become a regular part of parish meetings instead of the usual quick prayer and "getting down to business." Some parish workers who may not immediately desire to become a praying community might be open to a yearly evening of reflection. Increasingly larger numbers of people, however, will choose to directly and consciously become members of basic communities. Parishioners with different parish involvements will make choices as to which group will serve as their primary support community without negating their participation in other groups.

Parish Councils offer us an excellent tool to bridge the gap between our present institutional church and our communal model. Councils as we know them today have been in large measure an accommodation to provide participation in large and unwieldly parishes or smaller parishes that are not communal in nature. As we move forward, however, councils may provide the means for the parish to become a community of communities.

In truth it must be said that the average parish council today has not achieved a large degree of success. History will record, however, that councils were highly effective in helping priests, religious and lay people to learn to work together.

One of the greatest weaknesses of councils is that they usually draw their membership from elections at large, and winning candidates frequently have not benefited from a formation process that prepares them for responsible council participation. Unclear regarding the mission of the church and planning procedures, such councils have often opted for dealing with the parish finances or administrative matters. Even in those parish councils that have drawn their people from various areas of the church's mission, most members have not had adequate experience in a base of real community.

In retrospect, we have come to realize that most parish councils have been developed in reverse order. The structure was established before the people were developed to run them. Basic communities, therefore, offer an opportunity to correct this malady and vitalize councils by being a resource for both ideas and people. In the future I can envision up to 80 percent of council membership being drawn from small ministerial communities (where people have been formed) while still allowing for significant at-large representation. Indeed, this at-large representation would appropriately serve the interests of those people who continue to prefer the institutional model of parish.

The following diagram illustrates how this style of parish council would look.

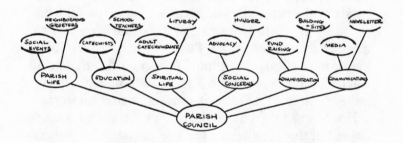

While this diagram should more appropriately be viewed as a circle, it is purposely shown in this line fashion to illustrate the diversity of activity feeding into the council. And because each input is based on small group formation, the council would be built on a solid grassroots foundation.

The key to this development, of course, is predicated on the growth occurring in the basic communities. As these communities become formed and active, they would nourish with both ideas and people the councils' standing committees. These committees themselves would become more communal in nature as they benefited from the experience of members who have had rich community backgrounds. The same process would be repeated, of course, in the relationships between "standing communities" and the council. The end result would be a strong communal model parish council that is better able to develop and implement the mission of the parish.

Another important advantage is that it would also strengthen traditionally weak areas of parish council activity, such as social concerns. Under the communities concept, addressing justice issues would become as much the concern of good parishioners as are parish finances now. The farther we move from centering on the institutional parish model, the more unacceptable will be the "departmentalized" spirituality that emphasizes our present vested interests.

How long might it be before we see a significant degree of this type of evolution in parish life? The answer to that lies largely with priests and other parish staff persons, be they deacons, religious, or laity. The full appreciation of the impact small communities have on peoples' lives can truly be gained only from actual experience. Theory or lectures will not convince the parish staff person who fears or is anxious about more open relationships with parishioners.

Therefore, the decision to move out from the security of desk and rectory to the living room setting entails courage and determination—and a certain amount of risk. It means that the teaching role must be balanced with a willingness to share the pains, struggles and joys that are common in all spiritual journeys. However, parishioners will respond with new respect and affection for the parish staff person who assumes the role of enabler and opens new pathways for people to serve the Lord's call.

I am aware, of course, that it is not just priests but new full time ministers who also tend to burn themselves out, trying to "do it all" in providing all forms of direct ministry. Perhaps this is because there is an underlying subtle form of mistrust of lay parishioners who don't have the "proper" professional theological degrees and therefore "don't understand." In any event, I believe the future will find parish staff persons spending a much higher percentage of time in developing leadership skills among parishioners and in melding these leaders into appropriate small basic communities. Tomorrow's pastor won't feel less important because he or she hasn't done it all himself/or herself. Rather he/she will find great satisfaction in having enabled others to carry out Christ's mission.

How will this vision come to be? Can we expect these communal developments to automatically occur? Of course not. Nor should we, since to allow things to grow like Topsy is to court disaster. However, the many conversion experiences that have marked movements in recent years have raised people's expectations. As we move forward with small communities and other means in the future, these expectations will continue to multiply. The last state could be worse than the first if we give no thought as to where we are going with those expectations and how they are to be met.

Training for priests, staff persons and parish leaders will be most critical. Understanding of organizational development psychology and the acquiring of leadership skills will be more important than ever. Process and pastoral experience will need to be brought together in a workable manner. Unfortunately, too many parishioners today are still skeptical of linking planning processes and workshops on organizational development with church activity.

However, as Americans, our experiences speak to us. Given a successful example of what parish life can be, I am confident people will be much more open to the planning process and acquiring the skills necessary to make their new visions come to reality. It goes without saying that parish planning procedures in the future will also be expected to show greater respect for research and to draw more heavily upon available data.

Community leaders will be required to undergo specialized training if they are to understand the stages of community development and the leadership needed for each. An awareness of basic group dynamics and fundamental theology of the Catholic Church are needed as starters. Leaders will also need to know their roles and relationships with regard to emerging parish vision, as well as insights into pastoring their special communities. In turn, the need for organizational training of parish priests and parish staff people will be greater than ever.

On another level, these parish developments may often require diocesan assistance. Fortunately, there are available today many professional people who are both highly qualified with organizational skills and also thoroughly familiar with the workings of the church. On the other hand, they have not always been utilized properly. In this respect, whole diocesan structuring and future planning would benefit greatly from their services. The new style of parish life necessitates that special assistance be offered to priests and other parish leaders whose training in the past prepared them for a different manner of leadership. Such an investment in the future is imperative.

More dioceses will also have to acknowledge a shifting parish emphasis towards communal style in other ways. Diocesan offices and agencies will increasingly need to program and provide materials for small parish communities. It is not enough that a youth department provide dynamic weekend experiences; follow-through materials for small communities and training for their leaders will be necessary. Religious education offices can bring young couples into mainstream parish life by offering the option of small community materials for sacramental preparation. Couples that opt for meeting in small groups with other couples in preference to instruction classes may well form lasting bonds of friendship and be a new source of parish leadership. Education offices also have the opportunity of calling people into new relationships and forms of parish life. Teachers who come together in communities of prayer and faith-sharing may, in their classrooms, well prove the old adage that "faith is caught, not taught."

Technological advances will also make their impact, and we must keep abreast of new communication and other tools that can be used to further the Church's mission.

The near future will continue to see more and more deacons, sisters, brothers and lay persons in the role of pastor. There will be a trend for priests to live in residences separate from their parish. A number of priests living in community may serve an even greater number of parishes.

The theme here is that people living in a society exploding outward into ever new dimensions will need even more to be rooted in communities supplying identification and support. If people today have difficulty orienting themselves to change, then the future —with its promise of even faster change—will bring an even greater urgency for people to be strengthened by bonds of supportive relationships that are centered in the unity of commonly shared faith.

The future offers an enormous opportunity for the church. Universal in nature, the church will be the one institution that will be able to offer humankind a structure that nourishes people as persons while meeting their deepest hunger for God. In past centuries the church was the champion of civilization through the promotion of education and the arts. In the future the church will serve the human family by meeting its great need for community. Indeed, the present generation has a serious responsibility to prepare for the needs of the future. As numbers of people multiply and the universe expands, community will need to be strengthened and fostered through small meaningful personal components. Small will be seen as beautiful.

The small, parish-based communities of the future, far from being a sign of regression or retrenchment, will be seen as dynamic and forceful. They will help to eradicate a passive Catholic philosophy of "settling to cut our losses" or merely "reclaiming the alienated." Rather the future parish will be more hopeful and rekindle action directed at changing the face of the earth and recreating the social order. Small faith communities will provide more than membership in this movement. They will be dynamic in nature making people very much alive in union with one another and their God. This mutual support and dynamism will empower people to interact with society in effective ways instead of being engulfed by it.

The bishops at Vatican Council II in the Dogmatic Constitution on the Church noted "the special urgency" of the Church's task of bringing all the people to full union with Christ. Despite the passage of time since the document was written, we have no reason to believe that this urgency has been diminished.

Rather, as we look to the future, we are struck by the increased need to accelerate our efforts. We are confident that the small group concept will serve to make an important contribution to the accomplishment of the Church's mission and to encourage the relationship to Christ so essential for its achievement.

Notes

1. "The Parish: A People, A Mission, A Structure," a statement of the Committee on the Parish, November 1980—The National Conference of Catholic Bishops.
2. Ralph A. Keifer, "Christian Initiation: The State of the Question"—*Made, Not Born* (Notre Dame, University of Notre Dame Press, 1976), p. 138.
3. Blaine G. Barr, "How Can a Large Parish Become a Viable Catechumenal Community?" *Becoming a Catholic Christian* (Sadlier).

Chapter Three

STRUCTURE

by James Hitchcock

WHEN asked to express his hopes for the Second Vatican Council in 1962, the novelist Evelyn Waugh wrote an essay entitled "The Same Again Please." In a sense that prescription can stand for a realistic appraisal of what the Church as an institution will be like by the beginning of the twenty-first century.

Nothing now seems as dated as those imaginative projections of the future sketched out by optimists of fifty or seventy-five years ago, in which cities existed under glass domes insuring perfect climate, every citizen owned a mini-airship for instantaneous travel about town, all disease had been vanquished, and poverty was unknown. All equipment of living— clothes, furniture, buildings, vehicles—were of recognizably ultra-modern design, streamlined in such a way that no trace of the cumbersome past remained.

Not only has such a future not been realized, nor is it likely to be, but relatively few people would now want it. Not only do we find much of the past worth saving, especially buildings and furniture, but we question the cost—in energy, in use of material, in alienation from nature—which would make such a life possible.

All prognostications of the future reflect either the desires or the fears of the prophet, and as such are suspect. The "science" of futurology seems to consist largely (as with its high priest, Alvin Toffler) of sketching out a prospect as the "scientist" would have it, then attempting to bring it into being by persuading people to expect it and to behave accordingly.

That this is true with respect to the Catholic Church is obvious. There is no more effective spur to changed behavior than persuading people that if they do not change they will be run over by the engine of history, and many reformers have been using this technique on bishops, for example, with some degree of success. In history, however, very few things are inevitable, and those who talk about inevitability are usually attempting to enforce change through panic.

Those who have not been paying full attention to what is happening in American religion in recent years can be forgiven for supposing, as many of them seem to, that the only religions with a future are the self-consciously "updated" ones. A liberal theology, a permissive morality, a modern style of worship, a leftist social doctrine—these describe the kind of church that modern Americans can take seriously.

The facts, however, are almost the reverse. It has been the liberal churches fitting the above description which have been declining in terms of members, while those churches which can be called conservative and even fundamentalist have been growing. The Catholic Church, in terms of membership, has been virtually stuck on dead center.

The reasons for this are complex and not altogether understood. Basically they seem to have to do with the fact that what people seek in religion is some understanding of the meaning of existence. The liberal churches seem very uncertain as to its meaning and seem to have no notion of faith other than following the spirit of the age. There are many people who would literally not be caught dead inside a conservative church. However, most of them are not joining the liberal churches either, simply because they see no need for religion at all. It seems reasonable, therefore, to expect that by the year 2000 most of the healthy, organized, confessedly Christian churches in America will be of the more conservative variety. The liberal churches will not so much disappear as metamorphize into something else. They will cease to call themselves churches and to proclaim the central significance of Christ. Nor will they see religion as their most important preoccupation.

The question of church structure cannot be considered apart from the question of meaning and belief, and one of the unfortunate side effects of the Second Vatican Council has been a tendency to tinker with structures without asking what they mean. In liberal circles it is common to make an unexamined distinction between the mere "institutional" church and the "real" church, with the implication that the former is unimportant, tends to interfere with the latter, and is subject to endless manipulation.

Yet the Council itself, in its decree on the church (*Lumen Gentium*, I, 8), denied the separation between the spiritual and institutional dimensions and affirmed that they are one. Thus before it is possible to project the plausible institutional shape of the future church, it is necessary to understand the church at its deepest level.

Put simply, the question is whether the church is indeed a divinely founded and divinely sustained institution. Catholics have been greatly influenced by liberal Protestant theology in the past twenty years, but often it has been assumed that this influence is piecemeal only. The church modifies its "rigid" teachings on certain points—sexuality, liturgical practice, eucharistic presence, for example—while the core of faith remains unchanged.

But the ultimate thrust of liberal Protestant (and now liberal Catholic) theology is precisely towards the final obliteration of all belief in the supernatural, of transcendent divine reality erupting into the mundane world, of an authority outside of and infinitely above humanity itself. In this view, which is only now becoming altogether candid, the Scriptures are a human book, inspired in a sense but not differently from the way in which Shakespeare is inspired. The Scriptures even contain pernicious falsehoods ("sexist" ideas, for example). The church, too, is a merely human creation, and it, too, has therefore been a vehicle for much evil and falsehood throughout history. Religious doctrines are emanations of the human mind and imagination, of greater or less degree of profundity. But all of them should be understood as merely among the ways in which man seeks to understand and interpret the universe. None of these doctrines should be understood as referring to transcendent realities. Much less should they be understood as directly inspired by God.

It follows, of course, that if the church is viewed in this way, there is no reason its structures cannot be endlessly molded and remolded, new ones put in place and old ones summarily discarded. Indeed there is no reason why the Catholic Church need remain the Catholic Church. It could transform itself into something else, as a company manufacturing potato chips, for example, might through a series of mergers and acquisitions come to be a "conglomerate" far removed from its original character.

If, however, the traditional Catholic doctrine of the divine origin and inspiration of the church is taken seriously, if the very idea of divine revelation is taken seriously, then the structure of the church in the twenty-first century will not be essentially different from what it is now and has been for nearly two millenia.

The basic structure is the tripartite one of episcopacy, priesthood, and laity. Although there is much debate as to the structure of the church in New Testament times (for which the evidence is extremely slender and much is speculative), there is no doubt that this tripartite division came to be normative very early in the church's history and has been so ever since. The letters of St. Ignatius of Antioch, not long after the year 100, attest to this.

Those who would "demythologize" this structure can only point to one seemingly significant historical deviation—in Ireland during the "dark ages" c400-900 the chief ecclesiastical figure was the monastic abbot, who governed the church in a particular area even though he was not a bishop. There were bishops, whose function was to administer the sacraments, but they had little governing authority.

The very fact that bishops were maintained at all in this society is testimony to their recognized importance, since otherwise it would have been natural for the abbots to have absorbed all episcopal functions. That fact plus the extreme rarity of the case, occurring in a part of the Church largely cut off from the rest of the Christian world, tends merely to emphasize the necessity of bishops. Just as the Second Vatican Council affirmed the unity of the institutional and spiritual dimensions of the church, so the separation of the sacramental episcopacy from the government of the church betrays a shallow understanding of the mystery of the church. Governance is not something imposed on the surface. For the church to be properly governed, its government must flow from its deepest springs, hence must be united to its sacramental reality, which the bishop expresses most fully. For someone to have power in the church simply for pragmatic reasons—that he is efficient, or because otherwise things would get disorganized—would be a perversion of the idea of Christian authority. The bishop has such authority primarily because he is the fullest representative of Christ to his diocese, and he mediates Christ to his people sacramentally.

Since the Council, bishops have become somewhat more conspicuous, in that it is now thought appropriate that bishops go among their people as much as possible, and the remote and olympian bishop is a disappearing type. However, in another way the most important thing that has happened to the episcopacy over twenty years has been a narrowing of the bishop's actual governing role. Diocesan bureaucracies have grown enormously, and one by one various episcopal responsibilities—finance, education, charity, liturgy, assignment of priests—have been taken over by specialists, with the bishop in many cases retaining only a nominal authority to approve or veto.

To a degree this has been necessary, because of the size and complexity of modern church government. But it is a process which has also gone too far, in that the bishop can become a kind of figurehead. When questioned, most Catholics say they want their bishops to be spiritual leaders. This presumably means, among other things, that they want bishops who are more conspicuous for the strength of their faith than for their financial acumen. It is a priority which in the past has perhaps not always been kept straight.

But it would also be unfortunate for the church if

the day came when the temporal administration of a diocese were entirely divorced from its spiritual leadership. The result would be an unfortunate ecclesiastical schizophrenia. The material concerns of the church are validated by its spiritual purposes. Hence it remains crucial that the ultimate spiritual leadership of the diocese also retain final authority over its temporalities. The same principle is even more true with respect to things like religious education and liturgy which are an integral part of the church's spiritual life. No bishop can legitimately consign these things entirely to "experts." If anything, the trend of the next twenty years is likely to be towards bishops who reclaim more of the governing authority given away, often inadvertently. The bishop of the future will have to be an extraordinary man precisely because he must not only master a great variety of tasks, he must also integrate them through a profound and powerful sense of his sacramental calling. Diocesan bureaucracies will not disappear, but they may decline in size and importance.

Something similar may happen at the parish level. Here, too, there has been a tendency for priests to become less reserved, hence more visible and even intrusive in parish life, while at the same time more parish responsibilities are taken over by others. For the most part this is to the good—there is no reason why a pastor should devote most of his working hours to finance or to problems of building maintenance, for example, if there are competent parishioners able to undertake those tasks.

But the same kind of fragmentation of authority has occurred in parishes as has occurred in dioceses. There are parishes where the school is so completely the domain of the educators who teach in it, for example, that the pastor has no voice in its operation, and what is preached from the pulpit may even be at odds with much of what is taught in the school. There are parish liturgy committees which operate with little or no priestly guidance.

None of these things—from the preparation of the Sunday liturgy to the remodeling of the school building, to the criteria for what kind of financial support is expected from parishioners—can be divorced from the sacramental life of the parish, of which the priest is the central figure. In the "new church" the pastor's role is in fact more demanding and central than before, because he must integrate great diversity into that sacramental life.

Here in particular the principle articulated earlier is relevant—the institutional dimensions of church life cannot be separated from the spiritual and sacramental. For example, when a parish debates its budget, priorities are involved which imply theological questions. (Should more money be put into the school, or is traditional religious education outmoded? Is it proper to air-condition the church when many needy people go unaided?) Disputes between pastor and teachers over what is taught in the school are likely to stem from theological disagreements. Liturgical practice obviously has immediate sacramental significance. None of these questions can merely be settled on the principle that responsibility has been given to particular people, who thereby become autonomous. The pastor may not be right, but as long as he is pastor he represents the fullness of the church's sacramental life in a way that no one else does.

In the next decade, with strong papal leadership, the disputed doctrinal questions which divide the church are likely to be settled, at least in the sense that official teachings will be clarified and emphasized and those in positions of authority will be expected to follow them. If this happens many of what at present appear to be jurisdictional disputes will evaporate, because they are really disagreements over belief itself.

Many people have interpreted the thrust of the Council as towards greater democracy in the church, with the corollary that lay people should now have more voice and power. But there is little in the conciliar decrees which bears this interpretation. The role of the laity is indeed emphasized, but almost always in terms of their apostolic mission in the world. The fact that the laity, too, share in the priesthood of Christ is indeed affirmed, but no connection is made between that and church government.

This is not to say that lay people should have no voice in governance, merely that secular democracy is an inappropriate model. Lay people already play a conspicuous role in areas where they were rather rare twenty-five years ago, particularly the intellectual life. As already noted, the talents of lay people have come to be utilized both at the diocesan and the parish level, wherever they seem relevant.

Once the question is cast in terms of a drive for "democracy," however, everything is falsified. For that concept implies a power struggle and a principle of majority rule, neither of which is valid in church government.

Parish councils function well in many parishes. There are even diocesan councils, and their number may grow. Probably such quasi-representative bodies will become permanent features of the church in America. However, an effective parish or diocesan council presupposes a basic harmony between priest and people, both in personality and in belief. It also presupposes a mutual trust, so that the pastor does not feel his authority threatened nor the council its legitimate concerns thwarted. Hence the real question, once again, is not structure so much as doctrine. Where unanimity of doctrine exists, other disagreements are likely to be less than crucial.

In fact, some reformers now seem to operate less with a democratic model than with a quasi-anarchical one. Their concept of democracy is not that of the United States government but of the rather exotic New England town meeting. On the secular scene no one supposes that a city council can nullify the laws of a state, nor state legislatures act contrary to Federal law. Yet democratic zealots within the church would use local bodies like parish councils to legitimize practices and implied beliefs (with respect to the liturgy, for example, or the status of people married outside the Church) which are contrary to Canon Law and to official doctrine. Once the beliefs of the church are sufficiently clarified, the limits of permissible action at the local level will have been established, and much of the tension presently inherent in the concept of representative bodies will be relaxed.

But will dioceses and parishes as we know them survive into the next millenium? Unlike priests and bishops, they do not partake of divine foundation. But they have been normal to the life of the church for many centuries. Common sense suggests that they will survive, since territorial jurisdictions are one of the most basic modes of administration in the modern world. Most people probably prefer to attend their neighboring church rather than search for one that might be more congenial.

At the same time, these jurisdictions have been less rigidly enforced since the Council, and it will probably continue to be the case that people who want to "shop" for a parish will be permitted to do so. However, once again the trail leads back to doctrine, since most shopping is probably motivated by a desire to find the "right" kind of liturgy, or preaching, or religious instruction. The present rather chaotic situation with regard to all three will not continue indefinitely.

For a time it was predicted that parishes would wither away because people would find it more rewarding to attend worship with others like themselves—groups would gather on Sunday morning brought together by common occupations, shared beliefs about the church or society, condition in life (e.g., divorced), etc. To an extent this has happened, but not to the extent that reformers predicted. The highly touted "underground church" seems to have largely disappeared, for many merely a way station on the road to secularity. There are still extra-parochial, unauthorized worship communities, as of militant feminists, but they seem unlikely to encompass more than a small minority of the total church and, since they seem to depend on the alienated, have only tenuous relationship to the church at large and not much durability.

The number of dioceses in America has been growing ever since the first one was established in 1789. There are many advantages to having smaller dioceses, especially given the bishop's crucial role as unifier of his see.

The number of parishes has also been growing, but their proliferation is limited by the substantial financial investment needed to start a new one, particularly in buildings. (A new diocese can designate an existing church as its cathedral, and its need for office space is not necessarily great.) Many people suggest, however, that church buildings are unnecessary, nor is it necessary to have a resident priest in each parish. Certainly there is no fundamental theological objection to either proposition. However, both do imply certain rather drastic alterations in the way Catholic life has been lived in this country (the liturgical implications of not having churches are especially important), so that a good deal more thought needs to be given to both proposals.

But what about the priest shortage? Already in some places it is acute. Based on present projections, by the year 2000 it will be all but universal.

This is a classic instance of the way in which administrative problems cannot be dealt with on the basis of administration alone. If revolutions in church practice are to take place, they should at least take place as a result of conscious decisions, and after sufficient reflection. Already, however, the prospect of a priest shortage has led to a situation in which the concept of "lay ministries" has been expanded without such reflection. Some people consciously promote them so as to effect a kind of revolution. Others merely accept them as a pragmatic necessity. But the implications of non-ordained persons administering communion on any but an emergency basis go deep. The custom in some places of letting lay people or religious discharge almost all functions except that of the Consecration of the Mass itself raises disturbing questions, in the real world, about whether priests are even needed. The symbolism of the priest as a kind of ritual functionary whose role is narrow and cultic only is precisely the wrong kind of symbolism to convey at the present time.

In God's providence there may yet be an increase in priestly vocations. If not, the important questions raised by their lack will have to be thought out very carefully, not dealt with piecemeal. If the number of priests does not increase, it is unlikely that parishes will be subdivided except in response to population growth. The condition of priestless parishes is one the Church will not want to foster except where unavoidable.

Will the shortage of priests mean the ordination of women and an end to required celibacy? The answer to the first part of the question is clearly no. It is formal papal teaching, hardly likely to be reversed, that women cannot be ordained. The question of married priests is more speculative. It is unlikely that celibacy will be waived as a condition for ordination among the young. To do so would be to imply that the Church no longer asks its priests to make this full witness for the Kingdom. However, it seems likely that the practice of ordaining mature married men may grow; it is already cautiously begun with respect to convert clergy from Episcopalianism.

The future of religious life also seems in doubt at present. This is not only because of the vocation crisis but also because of a basic uncertainty within religious communities about their very nature. The crisis is most acute and most visible in communities of women, which have gone from being the most rigid to the most trendy groups in the Church within a remarkably short period of time.

Self-definition seems crucial to the future of these communities. Although reliable statistics are hard to come by, there is definite evidence that the most "up to date" religious orders (especially among women) are attracting very few new members and have the

highest rate of attrition among older members. On
the other hand the more traditional orders are attracting a considerable number of novices, although
not as many as previously. The issue here is analo-
gous to the statistical pattern with respect to liberal
and conservative churches indicated previously—
there is little reason why anyone should join a community that seems to have no strong sense of its own
purpose and spirit and whose members seem to follow mainly their own inclinations.

Thus by the year 2000 practically the only viable religious orders in the Church will be the more traditional ones. The others will have largely disappeared.

Religious orders have been heavily involved in
America with religious education, and Catholic
schools, from nursery schools to graduate schools,
have been so conspicuous a feature of American Catholicism that some question must be asked about
their future.

The great majority of presently Catholic colleges
will have ceased to be so by the year 2000. Some have
already officially secularized; many have gone out of
existence. Most of those remaining give some indication of a desire to retain their religious heritage.
However, the process of secularization is inexorable
in most of them, as the number of religious on the
faculty sinks towards the vanishing point and as
fewer and fewer of the lay faculty are people with a
principled commitment to the school's stated religious character. A few institutions with substantial
financial resources will be able to retain a strong re-

ligious presence. Most will not. At best, Catholicism, on most campuses, will be confined to theology departments and campus-ministry programs.

Here, however, the emergent layman makes his presence felt significantly. A handful of neo-Catholic colleges have been established in recent years, most of them lay-run. Some of these at least will prove viable and may grow to become major institutions. In time religious will become more involved in them.

The future of Catholic charitable institutions is, like that of Catholic colleges, uncertain, and from similar causes—the decline of the religious communities operating such institutions, a loss of identity and purpose, and to some extent a desire for government funding which imposes a kind of secularization. However, Catholic hospitals, retirement homes, etc., are for the most part not as badly eroded as are the colleges and universities. Some of them are operated by religious orders which have retained a strong sense of identity and a viable community life. By the year 2000 there will probably be fewer such institutions than there are now, but they will still be a conspicuous presence.

Just after the Council it was freely predicted that parochial schools would disappear, and the forecast was an excellent example of prophecy designed to effect what it foretold. By now few people think parochial schools will disappear completely. Their number has declined sharply over fifteen years, but they seem to have reached a plateau.

Parochial schools have gained new popularity

from an unexpected source—liberals, including many blacks and some non-Catholics, who recognize that they are more effective than the public schools in many instances, and who use them as an alternative to the public schools.

Thus there is a danger that the parochial schools will pass away from success rather than failure—they will cease to be Catholic simply by changing into non-denominational private institutions.

However, the importance of parochial schools precisely as religious is stronger now than ever, as it comes once again to be recognized that education cannot be conducted simply on a technical basis but needs a moral and spiritual heart. As parents come to recognize this more and more, distinctly religious schools will gain a new strength. Indeed, one of the ironies of the past decade has been the fact that as Catholics have been closing their schools, Protestants have been opening more of their own, which in some cases may be due to racism but more often seems to express disillusionment with the utter secularism of public education.

The survival of Catholic education at the elementary and secondary levels seems, therefore, mainly to depend on good will and commitment. Such education is expensive, especially given the decline of teaching orders of sisters. But the American Catholic community is by and large prosperous and can afford those things it regards as worthwhile.

Any forecast of the shape of the Catholic Church

of the future obviously depends in large measure on some estimate of who will belong to that church. Here the evidence is susceptible of two opposite interpretations.

Conventional wisdom holds that the trends of modernism, in all aspects of culture, are too strong to be resisted. Thus the only religions which will have credibility in the year 2000 will be those which are streamlined and secularized to a significant degree, and especially those not wed to traditional dogma.

That there is a large population of secularized people there can be no doubt. For various reasons, especially the kind of church in which they grew up and the kind of religious education they were given, there is a large body of nominally Catholic young people (roughly those born between 1945 and 1960) who seem permanently alienated from the Church.

But, as already noted, there is also a strong trend towards conservative, even fundamentalist kinds of religion, probably for some of the same reasons people become secularized—opposite responses to the same cultural conditions. "Trends" are of their very nature superficial and not long-lasting. But if the religious sense is basic to human beings, then this pattern is likely to prove more than ephemeral.

The secularizing trends of the past twenty years have been stimulated to a great extent by artificial forces—a euphoric sense of release from all constraining social bonds. In the late 1970s many people started coming down to earth, a descent which led to a new willingness to ask basic questions about life's meaning. This inevitably leads to religion and to a reconsideration of eternal truths carelessly discarded.

Between now and the year 2000, the Catholic Church may experience a great surge of evangelization, with a concomitant increase in membership. However, judging from present trends it may just as well show a smaller membership than at present.

This will be for two reasons, if in fact this happens. One is that many people now see no good reason for maintaining largely nominal membership in a church whose teachings they do not accept. A generation which was raised in an intensely Catholic environment which made it difficult ever to give up the faith completely will give way to a generation whose religious upbringing was confused and superficial and who will easily drift away from the church of their youth. It is here that the fallacy of the liberal religious strategy lies—few such people are likely to be won to the church no matter how "open" it shows itself. They are simply not interested.

However, it may also be the case that membership in the Catholic Church declines as the church recovers a firmer sense of its self-identity. The full meaning of the Second Vatican Council has never been manifest, mostly because its message was misinterpreted in various ways (one of them being the structural tinkering referred to above, another the notion that what the Council proclaimed was that people are now free of all previous constraints). As that message is gradually clarified, many people will come to see that their impressions of what "renewal" is all about were mistaken. There are some rather active Catholics whose relationship to the church since the Council has been largely defined in terms of a series of "breakthroughs" against previous teachings and practices. Ultimately such people reach the end of this artificial stimulation, and when they confront the basic question why they should be Catholics at all they can find no satisfactory answer. Meanwhile a new generation not plagued by this ambivalence approaches those teachings with a fresh eye.

So far nothing has been said about the most conspicuous feature of Catholic Church structure—the Papacy. This is not because it is unimportant. Indeed, its importance is all-encompassing.

One of the tricks which history has played on confident progressives was the election of John Paul II. It was a trick because many people assumed the continuing decline of the prestige and influence of the papacy, and were suddenly confronted by one of the most formidable popes of modern times. By the sheer power of his personality John Paul insures that papal authority will not only endure but grow. He may still be pope when the third Christian millenium begins.

No council can nullify the solemn pronouncements of another council, and the Second Vatican Council hardly reversed the doctrine of papal infallibility as proclaimed by the First Vatican Council. Indeed, some of the strongest statements about papal authority come from the former. (See *Lumen Gentium*, III, 18, 22). The doctrinal basis of papal authority is beyond dispute.

Since the Council, there has been much discussion of the ways in which legitimate local diversity can be permitted and even encouraged in the church. While most of this discussion has centered on the Third World, there has also been talk about an "American Church."

What is usually not realized is that diversity among local branches of the universal church precisely requires a strong papacy, not a weak one, for otherwise diversity would quickly degenerate into chaos. All effective unity would be lost. The papacy is not only a symbol of unity but the principle by which that unity is maintained. This in turn implies strong teaching and disciplinary authority.

Some Catholics accept the papacy itself but not the papal curia, which they characterize as undermining genuine papal authority. There may be times when curial action (or inaction) does that. However, common sense dictates that a huge world-wide organization like the Catholic Church cannot be governed except through a large bureaucracy. The major problem, as at the diocesan level, is how that bureaucracy can be made an instrument of the church's sacramental mission. The Roman Curia now displays a great deal more ethnic and national diversity than was the case twenty years ago. Probably that trend will continue. Quite possibly the structure of the Curia will be altered, as has also occurred since the

Council. However, there is little doubt that the Curia itself will continue to exist.

The Pope is not simply the head of a large multi-national organization, and his authority does not stem merely from the need to have someone in charge. For it is in the person of the Holy Father that the "institutional" and "spiritual" dimensions of the church are unified fully, and their oneness manifested to the world. It is he who maintains unity within diversity, permanence amidst change, the spiritual within the temporal, a passion for worldly justice in the light of eternity, orthodoxy without rigidity, ecumenical openness with no sacrifice of truth, a love which is not sentimentally permissive but liberating and transforming, calling mankind to that higher level of existence which is its true Christian vocation.

Chapter Four

PRIESTHOOD

by Andrew M. Greeley

THE present state of the priesthood is marked by two pervasive conditions:

1) A loss of nerve among many priests as a result of the failure of confidence in the importance and uniqueness of their work.

2) An attempt to capture some importance for their vocation by redefining themselves as social activists instead of religious leaders.

As a result of these two situations, the conventional wisdom is that the priesthood of the future will be very different from the priesthood of the past. In years to come, it is said, the typical priest will be a part-time, married worker, ordained by the people of his community and he, in all likelihood, will be a she. The institutional church, like the socialist state, will wither away, and the part-time, married women priests responsible only to the local congregation will be the characteristic Catholic clergy.

Such was the vision of the priesthood espoused by the sometime Monsignor Ivan Illich in an article in *The Critic* many years ago, an article which had influence in notable disproportion to its intelligence. Illich's vision of the priesthood is both bad theology and bad sociology. Since, however, most of the leaders of the American priesthood—delegates to the meetings of the National Federation of Priests' Councils and the conference of major religious superiors of men—do not know much theology or sociology, the myopic and minimalist vision of the future of the priesthood is likely to continue. In fact, however, the future of the priesthood will be very different from what these blind men, who are leaders of the blind, imagine. One does not project into the future from a trend line established five years ago. Rather one projects from a much longer historical base. Such projection, of course, is impossible for those who are even more illiterate about history than they are about theology and sociology. Nevertheless, if one wants to know what priests will do in the twenty-first century, then one must ask what priests did in the first century, the eleventh century, the seventeenth century, the nineteenth century, and the early twentieth century. If one asks those questions and investigates those base points, then one would conclude that the priesthood of the future will be very much like the priesthood of the past—for the most part, made up of full-time, unmarried men (and perhaps, eventually, full-time, unmarried women).

The theological grounds for the loss of nerve among priests are to be found in the mistaken conviction of some theologians that the only way one can persuade the laity of their religious importance is by restraining and minimizing the role of the clergy. There has grown up since the Vatican Council a theology of the priesthood (with little in the way of historical documentation) that reduces the priest to a Mass-sayer and an absolution-giver, and virtually eliminates his long historical role as the religious leader of the community. In fact, a more careful study than that in which these theologians have engaged would even eliminate the need for a priest as an absolution-giver, since the laity gave absolution for at least 1300 years of Catholic history.

This minimalist theology, practiced even by such greats as Edward Schillebeeckx and Hans Kung, has had tremendous appeal among the anti-clerical lay pseudo-intellectuals who dominate liberal Catholic journals and minister in turn to the self-hatred of the clergy. It has also been reinforced by the emergence of the so-called "new ministries" in Catholic life—youth minister, director of religious education, etc., etc., etc. With "youth ministers" and "DRE's" and "parish staffs," the typical nerve-losing parish clergyman says, "There's nothing left for us to do, nothing distinctive but our robes, we are a vanishing breed."

Under such circumstances, it is understandable perhaps that priests through their national leaders turn to the cheap grace of instant social action militantism. Thus, establishing the truth of Greeley's (Third) Law: There is an inverse relationship between the vitality of an institution and the militancy of its social action rhetoric. This law, which also can be called the law of Catholic organizations, can be rephrased simply as "the more relevant the rhetoric, the more irrelevant the organization," and can be expressed even more bluntly with the following words: certain evidence that an institution is about to liquidate itself is that those presiding over the liquidation will inform leaders of other institutions how to resolve their problems.

Thus, the conferences of major superiors of men assembles at a time of the greatest crisis in Western Catholic religious life since St. Benedict and passes ringing resolutions against the neutron bomb, the defense budget, Reagan economics, and American involvement in El Salvador, and vigorously endorses both gun control and the ERA.

No one in his/her right mind would think that these long lists of militant resolutions would change the vote of one congressman or even the mind of one Catholic. Indeed, they won't even change the mind of one member of the religious communities represented at the meeting. But they do provide the religious leaders with a way of feeling good as the walls come tumbling down around them. Vocations, direction, morale, vision—all of these apparently are to be ignored if only one can equate the work of one's Holy Founder with contemporary, social action fads. The successors of Francis and Dominic and Ignatius and Benedict and Jean Jacques Ollier have been reduced to repeating the warmed-over cliches of year-old editorials in the *Nation* or the *Christian Century* or the *Washington Post*.

And their counterparts at the National Federation of Priests' Councils, having been told that the most important influence on the religious life of Catholics is the quality of Sunday preaching, and that 80 percent of the Catholics in the country gave the clergy low marks on preaching, wanted to talk not about how they improve the quality of their homily, but rather about the problems of Latin America. As one priest, in as sublime a statement as one can imagine of the idiocy currently affecting the presbyterate, put it, "The whole world is my parish, not merely the people that listen to me on Sunday."

It did not occur, apparently, to this absurd man that he had little chance of influencing the whole world and considerable chance of influencing his parishioners. Nor that his parishioners pay his salary so that he minister the word of God to them. Nor that having failed in his obligation of strict justice to preach the Gospel well to them, he was a hypocrite, a whitened sepulchre if he preached about justice anywhere else in the world.

In the short run, the blind fools will remain with us and will do a tremendous amount of harm. They may indeed be responsible for the liquidation of the religious orders of men in the United States as we now know them and for a considerable diminishment of the size of the diocesan presbyterate. However, with no understanding of the past and no comprehension of the present, these men at best will have a negative influence on the future. They are lost explorers perishing in the wilderness instead of the pioneers of the new humanity as they imagine themselves.

I will leave to others the refutation of the naive theology of the priesthood which creates what passes for virtue in the contemporary American presbyterate, and content myself with sticking to my own loom of social science.

First of all, the priesthood is the only profession that I know of that tries to define itself not only without any regard for those who are its role opposites, but indeed without considering that any useful input at all might be made by the ordinary clergy. Priests are what priests say they are and the laity had damn well better be satisfied with that. In fact, all the empirical evidence shows that the laity still regard priests as religious leaders and still want full-time priests, preferably (though not necessarily) celibate. The data also show the enormous importance in the religious life of the church of such traditional priestly activities as preaching and counseling and finally demonstrate that when the clergy begin to preach about social justice—their newest amusement—the laity promptly turn them off because of their conviction that on such matters the clergy are no better informed or no more useful as guides than they are when they speak about the rules appropriate for married sexuality.

The priest, in other words, is as important as he ever was in the church, and probably more important because the laity look much less to the bishops and to the pope for leadship than they did twenty years ago. Indeed, the most important people in the religious life of a Catholic lay person are that person's spouse and that person's parish priest—note well, not youth ministers, or directors of religious education, or any of the other currently fashionable additions to the parish staff. If priests want to believe that their ministry is less important because of the development of the "new ministry" and because of the emergence of a new theology of the laity, there is nothing much that one can do to change that belief. At least they ought to be told, insistently and repeatedly, in season and out of season, that there is extremely powerful empirical evidence to the contrary.

How can it be that the laity, who pay the bills, can have such a completely different picture of the importance of priestly ministry and of traditional priestly occupations such as preaching and counseling than do priests themselves?

Part of the answer to this question, I am convinced, is the arrogance of priests. I use the word arrogance here in a carefully delimited sense: the assumption by priests that because they are priests they know all that there is to know and all they need to know on any given subject. The old a priori scholastic, philosophical and theological training in the seminary produced a presbyterate which thought it knew the answer even before the questions were asked. Scholasticism is dead but the serene self-confidence of the poorly educated clergyman that his own random ideas picked up on the morning news are the final word on almost any given subject has been little changed. There are few if any feedback mechanisms built into priestly ministry, not even a wife to tell you when you are making a damn fool out of yourself. Therefore, when a priest talks nonsense, he is likely to be greeted with silence (sometimes sullen silence, but after a while a priest becomes so insensitive to reactions to his foolishness that he doesn't even note how sullen the silence is). While priests have militantly advocated channels of communication by which they may speak upward to the bishops and the pope, they have paid little attention to building channels of communication beneath themselves through which the laity may express their view of things. In such a set of circumstances, then, the priest listens to those laity to whom he wants to listen and thus guarantees that his prejudices, preconceived opinions, and ridiculous biases are confirmed even before he listens.

Moreover, the changes in the church have by no means eliminated the authoritarianism of the clergy. Most priests still believe that they are the "boss" and since most people in the parish have better things to do than fight the parish priest, the pastor can still do pretty much what he wants. And indeed the modern, authoritarian, tyrannical pastor may even be more powerful than his predecessor because he has all the tricks of psychological gimmickry available to facilitate manipulation.

Thus, one of the finest parishes in the country was destroyed in a month by a new pastor who said all the right things but who drove the teenagers from the rectory, dictated what kind of clothes women should wear, lengthened the parish liturgy, and eliminated popular priests from the parish staff—all while mouthing the most approved pseudo-liberal clichés. He could get away with it of course because he had the piece of paper in his pocket from the chancery office. He was the pastor. It was his parish. He owned it, and he could do anything he damned well pleased. The authoritarianism and arrogance, then, of the clergy frees them from any need of listening to what the laity really need and want in their parish ministers. The fool who destroyed this parish was convinced that his role was to be the man who brought order and discipline and administered integrity to the community. The people wanted what they had had and what all the people wanted—priests who speak inspiringly and console sympathetically. But no one asked them, and no one is likely to ask them.

Sometimes I am convinced that the clergy do not want to hear of the importance of preaching and counseling because they know how bad they are at it and are afraid that they are incapable of improving. It is much easier to be an authoritarian administrator or a peace and justice pietist than it is to be a good preacher and a kind and sympathetic counselor.

What then will the priesthood of the future be like? If the laity have any say about it—and, since they pick up the bills, eventually they will—the priesthood of the future will be marked fundamentally and essentially by an enormous improvement in the quality of preaching and the quality of sympathetic listen-

ing. The arrogant, authoritarian administrator will
be replaced by men (and, please God, women) who
know how to listen sympathetically, encourage sensitivity, preach effectively, and console lovingly. There
may not be much difference between this ideal of the
priesthood and that which has existed for almost two
thousand years. Indeed, its "old fashioned" aspect
may discourage and depress and even affront those
who are convinced that that which is new is good
and that which is old can't possibly be good. Nonetheless, as a sociologist, I must state candidly and
bluntly that the preacher and the consoler, the poet
and the precinct captain are what the laity want in
their clergy, and I cannot imagine them not getting
what they want eventually—although the clergy's capacity to preach justice for everyone else in the
world and not practice justice towards their lay people is so profoundly structured into the priestly
worldview that the presbyterate may be able to hold
off its employers for a considerable period of time.

Will there be no structural changes at all? Will
priests in 2082 be doing pretty much the same thing
that priests did in 1082?

I'm inclined to answer that there will be rather few
structural changes and that indeed 2082 will look remarkably like 1082. People will still go to priests for
challenge and consolation. Priests will still preside
over the liturgy and preach the word of God, and
priests will still be the religious and to some extent
the social leaders of the Catholic community.

There may be some institutional changes. Hope-

PHILLIPS MEMORIAL
LIBRARY
PROVIDENCE COLLEGE

fully there will be women priests. But I do not believe that the ordination of women will affect the structure of the ministry anymore than the extension of the vote to women affected the structure of politics. In both cases, the changes are matters of justice but not institutionally transformative.

There are, however, two structural changes which seem to me to be worth mentioning: a much closer interaction on a social, personal and human basis between the clergy and the laity; and the development, first *de facto* and then *de jure*, of a limited service priesthood.

The conventional wisdom since the second Vatican Council has been that the priest ought to emerge from the secluded protection of the rectory and become a human like other humans. As my students at the University of Arizona have put it, "a priest should be as human as we are so he can understand all the problems that we suffer; but he should be a little bit better at dealing with those problems so that he can give us a model to imitate." The author of the Epistle to the Hebrews could not have put it better.

However, neither the clergy nor the laity have thought through, or indeed have thought at all about the problems of the heightened vulnerability of the priest once he becomes no longer the odd man in the rectory but the odd man out, the stranger, the third man, the one who does not fit in the ordinary life of the community. Since I believe that celibacy is likely to continue, I see the priest-as-odd-person to be a very serious problem for himself and for his lay peo-

ple until both sides are prepared to accept it and
even rejoice in the priestly oddity. However, at the
present time, all too many laity will insist, on the
one hand, on the need for human interaction with
priests, and on the other be threatened and terrified
if the priest continues to be disconcerting; that is to
say, if he continues to be an eschatological witness to
a world beyond this one and to a reality which transcends this one.

Most lay people, it seems to me, are perfectly de-
lighted with lap-dog priests that they can patronize
and protect and dominate, but they don't want
strong, tough priests who minister a gospel of para-
dox and challenge. By what they say, by what they
do, and by who they are, a very substantial number
of the clergy, it would seem, are only too content to
settle down to be domesticated pets who disconcert
only with radical social action rhetoric which, of
course, has no practical effect on peoples' lives.

One is reminded of the famous remark of novelist
Bruce Marshall to the Harvard intellectual who complained about the Irish priest in Boston. The clergyman, it seems, preached mostly on sexual sin and
rarely mentioned the sins of concentration camps, to
which Marshall replied that not very many members
of the parish in question were likely to commit a concentration camp—similarly not many laity are likely
to commit a neutron bomb or a multinational corpo-
ration. Hence, radical social action rhetoric is not
likely to be disconcerting to them at all.

The priest as-odd-person-out is one of the deepest,

most painful problems facing the church today and one which no one is willing to face, indeed, even address. Eventually, in the priests of the future, it will have to be faced.

Moreover, it seems likely that we will have in the years ahead a limited service priesthood. I do not mean the part-time priest who so delights Msgr. Illich and his admirers. I mean a full-time priesthood for a limited period of a person's life. A young man or a young woman will agree, for example, to commit five years of their life to the ministry of the priesthood (which will continue to be celibate). At the end of that period, they and church leaders will reconsider and another period of commitment might or might not be made. Precisely because one need not plan to be a priest until one dies, a much larger number of young people will experiment with a priestly career, and many of them, finding it both satisfying and challenging, will remain priests for a long period of time, if not indeed for their whole life and the result will be a much larger presbyterate than we have now and a solution to the priest shortage.

There are theological objections to this development, most of which seem to miss the point: that if one indeed is a priest forever, one need not be committed to the active exercise of the ministry forever. Such a permanent commitment to the priesthood in most eras before the last century probably only meant ten or fifteen years at the most, on the average. Now it means fifty years on the average. The church has not been able to comprehend the enormous difference that this demographic change makes and refuses to reflect on its theological implications.

However, practically do we not indeed have a limited term priesthood? The young men who are ordained in the 1980s know full well that leaving the priesthood is socially and religiously acceptable, if canonically somewhat more difficult than it was a few years ago. However, since few people take canon law seriously anymore, John Paul II's restrictions in granting dispensations from the priesthood are not likely to have much effect. We have, in other words, all the disadvantages of a limited service priesthood, with none of the recruiting advantages. I cannot imagine such a situation lasting for very long. So, entering the priesthood or leaving it could easily become a relatively simple career change and one which would greatly benefit the life of the church.

That's why nobody wants to talk about it presently. Much better to rant about the neutron bomb.

I should make clear by way of concluding parenthesis that I don't like the neutron bomb. As a matter of fact, I don't like the machine gun or gun powder either. I believe that in the future, priests will preach on social justice even as they did in the past. I trust that this future social justice preaching will be based, as it was in the past, on a far clearer understanding of the unique Catholic social theory which those who go to the NFPC and the CMSM meetings seem to have forgotten completely. I also presume that such deep and passionate concern, which has always marked the priesthood, for the poor and the oppressed of the world will not in the future be used, as it now is, as an excuse for not performing one's own professional obligations well. Priests in the future, I would submit, will rediscover that people will take them seriously when they speak about social concerns if they themselves are concerned about justice in their own ministry.

My emphasis then in this chapter is not against social action ministry in the future of the priesthood, but rather in favor of social action ministry that is professionally competent and well informed, that is steeped in traditional Catholic social theory and that is not a quick and easy substitute for the daily responsibilities of pastoral work—social action ministry, in other words, that is not "cheap grace."

The view of the priesthood expressed here is unfashionable and will, I fear, be unpopular, since it emphasizes continuity rather than change, tradition rather than revolution, a priestly ministry with which we are all familiar instead of one spun out of cotton-candy fantasies. Any serious and responsible consideration, it seems to me, of the trend lines set by the past and the present of the priesthood can only project a future in which priests will be doing pretty much what they've always done. This is not necessarily a conservative perspective, but an honest one.

Chapter Five

WOMEN

by Kaye Ashe

IN professing mystification about what women really *wanted*, Freud seemed to assume that there should by a tidy 10-point plan which would clear things up, but by now it should come as no surprise that women do not all think alike. Women in tomorrow's church, like the women in today's, will exhibit the same healthy pluralism that we take for granted in society at large. My reflections in this chapter represent one section in the chorus of women's voices being raised on church issues. They will be most relevant for women who have been touched by the women's movement. While these numbers in the church were small in 1970, they have grown at an astonishing rate in the intervening years. Among us also, however, there are differing views, goals, and hopes. This need not be a fact to deplore. Provided the dialogue remains open, the diversity of voices can result in sharper thinking and a surer movement toward the justice we proclaim for all in church or society.

It is undeniable that in the past ten years feminist analysis and action have sensitized the church to women's issues within the church,[1] but women who bring a strong sense of self and a high regard for their sisters to their study and experience of theology, liturgy and ministry continue to feel alienated amidst the patriarchal trappings of the institutional church. John Paul II, in his journeys of 1980, seemed determined to ignore women or to keep us on the margin, depriving us of even our legitimate role as extraordinary ministers at the functions surrounding his visit. The explanation that no lay people would serve as ministers (and that the exclusion was not, therefore, directed against women) was a transparent coverup. It underscored not only the still flourishing male/female hierarchy, but also the stubborn clerical/lay stratification so far removed from the ideal of mutuality and collaboration espoused by women in the church.

Women have gone far beyond simply cataloguing grievances of this kind, however. Indignation and frustration still swell, and protest is still made, but feminist scholars have laid bare the profound roots of this sort of exclusion. We have become aware of the dimensions of the problem, and recognize that superficial cosmetic surgery will not cure it. It will not be sufficient to introduce a few female nouns and pronouns into church language, nor to permit women to administer communion and to serve on parish teams. These reforms are helpful, but before women feel entirely at home in the church, profound psychological and structural transformations will have to take place. Some have judged the church incapable of the kind of change required and have moved out of institutional structures to continue their spiritual quest in Goddess worship or other forms of religious experience. Those who remain do so because they see in their church membership something more than adherence to a sexist (or racist, or classist) institution. They recognize in their parishes, dioceses and religious congregations a people struggling toward the justice and freedom and love proclaimed by the Gospel.

What will this struggle involve as far as women are concerned? What will the church of the future look like if women in the church who are working for change continue to make headway? The sketch that follows is based on trends that have grown stronger in the last ten years, and on some personal hopes. It is not meant to suggest that progress toward the implied goals is inevitable. Indeed, we cannot lose sight of the depressing possibility that the gains already made might be lost, as women's insights, writings and deeds have been lost in the past. But building on the scholarship, and on the ministerial and political experience that women in the church have attained in the last decade, and assuming that our creativity and vision will increase in breadth and depth in the decade to come, what changes can we, as women, hope for in the theology, liturgy, and ministry of the future?

Theology and Related Questions

Despite the condescension or derision with which women theologians were first met, and continue to be met in some circles, their careful dissection of

male-centered and male-dominated theologies has
exposed the oppressive character and the inade-
quacy of these traditions.

Thirteen years after the first eloquent and searing
charges made by Mary Daly in *The Church and the
Second Sex*, the search continues for concepts, language, symbols and rites that correspond to women's
new reading of themselves, their past, God, and the
universe. The spiritual quest goes on within and
without church structure.

Without pretending that there is consensus among
all of the women who have rejected patriarchal structures[2], I will summarize here certain convictions and
visions we share. Since feminist theologizing has already had an impact on the field, it is not hopelessly
naive to imagine that these convictions will enjoy
wider and wider currency in tomorrow's Church.

First of all, women in the last decade have come to
trust their own experience as a more reliable base for
an understanding of God than dogmas and belief sys-
tems that are the result of male cogitation and experience. Reliance on personal experience rather than on
authority is not new in the women's movement. Elizabeth Cady Stanton in the 19th century came more
and more to question the "experts" and to rely on her
mother wit and experience whether in caring for her
children or in interpreting the Bible. She, together
with a team of 22 scholars, produced a *Woman's
Bible*. The object was to comment upon texts and
chapters referring to women and to highlight pas-

sages in which women were conspicuously absent. They hoped thereby, as the editors note on the title page, ". . . to strip anti-feminism of its divine cloak."[3] Stanton's team was quick to realize that biblical texts were, like every other writing, influenced by historical factors and by the personal assumptions and cultural biases of those producing them. This was a crucial insight for pioneer feminists since the Word of God was often used to justify women's subjugation.

Stanton's approach to the Bible was too revolutionary even for some of her feminist friends, but today the notions of cultural relativity and historical criticism are taken for granted as principles of biblical interpretation. The realization by women that male experience and male perspectives have dictated theological, biblical and ethical language and principles has led us to re-read the Bible from our own experience and our own point of view, and to insist explicitly not only on the fact that theology is derived from experience, but to affirm human experience, female as well as male, as one basis for the development of theology, ethics, and hermeneutics. The idea is embraced now, of course, by theologians of both genders, but many men have difficulty with it. Naomi Goldenberg writes of a professor who asked her to leave the word "experience" out of any material she wrote for him because ". . . he did not understand what it meant."[4] And Father William Most lambastes the theologians writing in Leonard Swidler's *Consensus in Theology* because they dare to

claim that there are two sources which mediate
God's revelation to us: the Gospel and human experience.[5] He finds human experience messy, preferring,
no doubt, the kind of theology which pretends to rise
above experience, but which, in fact, is based on the
narrow range of experience of certain men.

But the move is on, and women in tomorrow's
church will be less and less patient with theologies
and authoritarian pronouncements which ignore or
belittle female experience. Those areas of Christian
tradition which are detrimental to women will become progressively weaker, and the whole Church
will be better off for it.

If women's experience is to shape the theology of
the future, old symbols, myths, and language will
gradually give way to ones which more truly reflect
women's lives, women's hopes and fears. This will
occur not through resolutions passed at bishop's
meetings or at feminist conferences, but through the
increased capacity of women to ". . . discover their
meaning, conceive their project, fulfill their service,
define their expectations, refine their attention, offer
their leadership, give their witness, formulate their
prayer, share their worship, create their life."[6]

Out of this expanded consciousness, out of this
new energy and power will be forged stories and
symbols which go beyond those of fathers and sons.
And the stories and symbols will be expressed in language that reflects these changes. Women and men
whose consciousness has already been changed do

not need directions about how to avoid sexist language. Their language adapts to a changed vision of what it means to be female, of women's place in society, and women's relationship to men.

The new vision leads to a reappraisal of images representing God and of the religious myths born from men's hopes and fears. God as patriarch and majestic Lord gives way to God our Mother and Father, to the God of Light and Life, God the Source of our Being, God the Spirit of Peace. The imaging of God exclusively in male terms has reinforced male authority, creativity, and prestige and has limited women's capacity to see themselves as God's image and to value their experience as revelatory of God's action. This capacity was not enhanced by the Vatican Declaration of 1977 which states that only males can adequately represent Christ in the offering of the Eucharist.

The effects on women of the absence of a female person in the Trinity (the Holy Spirit is not an unambiguous female principle) have been more subtle than the effects of the myth of the female prototype, Eve. The story has been re-read by women in the last decade, however, from women's point of view.

Most feminists have exposed the purposes which this myth has served, and buried it once for all. They perceive in the Eve of Genesis the primordial scapegoat who bears the burden of the fall from grace and comes to embody moral and intellectual incompetency, lust, and whatever other weaknesses men choose to externalize in women, thus leaving themselves strong and morally superior, and justifying their continued domination.

Phyllis Trible's approach has been different. She reclaims Eve by rejecting the interpretations visited upon her by men and by returning to the text with fresh eyes, this time female eyes.[7] She discovers an Eve who is intellectually more sophisticated than her mate, the one with whom the subtle serpent chooses to enter into theological dialogue. Eve is the more aggressive partner, and the one with greater sensibilities. She acts independently of her husband. "The man," writes Trible, "does not theologize; he does not contemplate; he does not envision the full possibilities of the occasion. His one act is belly-oriented, and it is an act of acquiescence, not of initiative." Her motive in the reinterpretation of the myth is not to promote female chauvinism, she explains, but to rid the text of patriarchal interpretations. Eve emerges from the reading as Adam's equal (at the very least!). The two enjoy complete physical and psychological rapport; they are equally responsible for the Fall and equally redeemed.

Because women have long since dealt with the Eve myth either by rejecting it or by exercising female hermeneutical privilege, it comes as a shock to come upon the cover of a parish bulletin[8] which features the names ADAM and EVE in large, bold print. The final "e" in Eve gives way in four transformations until the final version reads ADAM and EVIL. Lent is proclaimed on the same cover as a "journey of growth."

In the vain hope that the clergy might grow more sensitive to women's reaction to this blatant misogynism, some women protested. In one reply the pastor asked if his correspondent had ever requested the Lord to apologize for the passages in Genesis and the Epistle to the Romans that he inspired. His further defense of the cover was to point out that the "art work" was done by a man chosen by the Bishops to work on diocesan projects. Why quibble about the message, he seemed to suggest, when it's laid out so tastefully? On the same Sunday the homilist speculated as to why men would ever want to marry "used goods." The rage his remarks inspired in a recently remarried young widow carried her right out of the Church. She follows others who prefer to be considered evil by church fathers than to be "good" by their standards. These have come to the conclusion that religion is a male cult whose *raison d'etre* is to exclude women, and glorify male domination.

The contrast between women's reinterpretation of scripture and symbol and this recent sample of clerical clinging to readings which are degrading for women, is striking and disheartening. But it shouldn't suggest that the struggle is hopeless. At any given moment, both outmoded and future-oriented trends will exist within the Church. I believe, however, that more and more women in tomorrow's church will be less and less inclined to argue or plead or register protest with men in the Church whose lives suggest hopeless isolation in an all-male club where women exist principally to serve men's needs.

Rather, they will work with other women and with men who can collaborate as equals in research, liturgy, and ministry.

Liturgy

The Church's liturgy is a faithful mirror of its theology and scriptural interpretations. Women are still on the periphery in liturgical celebrations, conspicuously absent from the altar and pulpit although present in large numbers in the pews. Despite the call of women for a liturgical language which takes women into account, the pseudo-generic term "man" abounds in church sanctuaries, and hymns are still sung which refer exclusively to fathers, brothers, and brotherhood. Visual representations—statues, illustrations in missalettes, wall paintings, figures in stained glass windows—seldom give the same emphasis to women as to men. Homilies are sometimes used as excuses for attacks on feminist causes. They are often far removed from the reality of women's lives and appear to be addressed by men to men, or to women seen only in their relational roles of wife and mother. Women who attend liturgical services in some hope of confirmation of their aspirations or of their experience, often leave feeling empty or even demeaned.

Liturgies exist, however, in which women can feel at home. Once they are experienced, male-fixated liturgies become unpalatable. Consider the prayer events at the second Women's Ordination Conference held in Boston in 1978. Most were presided over by women, such as the first one held at the harbor. The presider greeted those present with the reminder that "2,000 years ago, a man from Galilee stood by a lake and invited the women and men in the crowd to be ministers. . . ."[9] Those present recalled their foremothers: Miriam, Judith, Mary, Priscilla, Joan of Arc, Teresa of Avila. God was addressed as Holy Spirit, as Creator, as Father and as beyond God the Father. The Prayers of the Faithful in the Eucharistic liturgy reflected the kinds of concerns that are close to women's hearts, although they are clearly not exclusively women's concerns: equality among all classes, sexes, and races, disarmament, an end to war, affirmation of reformers, prophets, preachers and poets, a restored planet and full table for our children's children.[10]

This conference, of course, was bound to be sensitive to women's needs; its liturgies were expressly designed to give expression to women's experience, sometimes painful in present church structures, and to suggest what will be possible in the Church of the future. They demonstrate that we do not need to wait for the ordination of women in order to have prayer services and liturgies in which women are visible, our voices heard, our viewpoint represented, and our leadership recognized.

The alternation of men and women (lay and religious) as planners of liturgies, preachers, extraordinary ministers, lectors, ushers, and eventually as deacons and priests will be the natural outgrowth in the area of liturgy to the expanding role of women in

Church and society; logical and natural, but not easy. Progress toward the goal will require continued encouragement of women by women, steady insistence on women's rights, continued education, and organized action.

Ministry

Women in the Church even now are engaged in a wider variety of ministries than ever before in the history of the Church. We preach, heal, counsel, and baptize. We work as liturgists, missionaries, assistant pastors, religious education coordinators, hospital and college chaplains, nurses, doctors, college faculty and administrators. But we are not always comfortable in these positions. Not because we are not qualified for them, but because the patterns of authority and power in the parishes, prisons, hospitals, and educational institutions within which we minister often frustrate our efforts. The words used most frequently by women when speaking of ministry are equality, mutuality, and collegiality. The call most frequently made is for a change in the power model. The call is not for a simple change of guard at top levels, thereby introducing more women into the corridors of church power, but for a dismantling of structures and an elimination of titles and costumes more appropriate to the Holy Roman Empire than to the church founded by Jesus. It is a call for the abolition of clerical caste and for the meaningful inclusion of the entire church in decisions affecting its membership.

Certain dioceses, parishes, and religious congregations are inventing new models of organization, ones which are participative rather than hierarchical, and which include groups formerly barred from any significant decision-making processes: women, minorities, and the economically poor. These are the models which conform to feminist philosophy. The chance that they will become more common in the church of tomorrow is not unrelated to the question of women's ordination.

The arguments used to justify the exclusion of women from priesthood are wearing thin. The weight of tradition, the historical fact that there has never been a woman priest does not settle the question. We must ask why women have been excluded in the past, and determine whether the same situation and the same factors obtain in our day. Tradition, after all, is a living thing. We must recall the historical facts of women's role in the early Church as deacons, as Paul's co-workers, as first witnesses of the Resurrection, and in the medieval Church as abbesses with quasi-episcopal powers. We must look squarely at the theological objections which have been proffered: the inferiority and subjection of women, the supposition that the mediating function of Christ can only be signified by the male sex, the supposed will of Christ ("If Christ had wanted women priests, he would have ordained his mother"), and decide whether they conform to the basic Gospel message and to our Christian experience.

Much work has already been done toward sorting

out the theological from the political, cultural, and sociological factors in the continued refusal to ordain women, and toward distinguishing God's plan from men's. Elizabeth Schüssler-Fiorenza, Anne Carr, Margaret Farley, George Tavard, Haye van der Meer, and Arlene and Leonard Swidler, among others, have contributed toward a theology which conforms to new insights into scripture and which paves the way for an ordained ministry of women and men. There are those who concede that there are no theological grounds for denying orders to women, but who wonder whether women priests would be accepted. We have all seen women themselves move out of a communion line leading to a female extraordinary minister in order to receive from "Father's" hand. This prejudice, however, cannot be seriously offered as a reason to refuse ordination to women. Rather than reinforce the prejudice by continued refusal to ordain women, should we not make every effort to dissolve it by careful preparation of our parishioners and by the witness of excellent women presiding at liturgies, preaching the Word, healing and reconciling?

That said, I must now admit that even while my heart and mind say "yes" to women priests, questions keep pushing their way into my consciousness. Will women in ordained ministry lose the freedom of movement, the versatility and the style of shared authority which have marked our ministry thus far? Or can we hope that instead of being absorbed into a priesthood which has not escaped elitism, arbitrariness, undue caution, and oppressive authoritarianism, our sisters will transform it? Or will the real transformation in priesthood be accomplished when the great chasm between ordained ministry and all other ministry is closed?

The issue is a complex one and does not admit of perfectly satisfying solutions. At this point in history, however, it is in the interest of the Church that women, lay and religious, occupy positions at every level of leadership, authority and service. As they attain these positions let us hope our sisters purge them of whatever remains of medieval custom and costume, of hierarchies which stifle rather than nourish, of a tendency to quarrel about ritual rather than reflect on the meaning of the Gospel, both its eternal, unchanging, transcendent aspects and its relevance in our neighborhoods, cities, nations, and universe. I am confident that even now the nature of ministry is changing by virtue of women's participation in it. But whether or not women's acceptance into ordained ministry would prove it, justice requires that women must no longer be barred from it for the simple fact that they *are* women.

More welcome even than the presence of women in pulpits and at altars will be the changed relationship between sexes which this implies, and the changed appraisal of women's "place" in the Church. Rather than rhapsodizing about woman's symbolic value and inestimable service to the

Church in certain prescribed areas, ordained ministers in the Roman Catholic Church will soon, I hope, welcome real women into their ranks. Then we can reflect *together* on one *another's* role, place, and ministry. Then together we can teach, preach, prophesy, learn, catechize, theologize, legislate, and celebrate the Word and the Eucharist.

Meanwhile much study and theologizing remains to be done on the nature and deepest meaning of priesthood, on its historical development and cultural anachronisms, as well as on the question of full participation of women in the Church. The process itself will be all the richer if the study and theologizing are done by both women and men in and out of orders. A recent and hopeful example of the sort of study and dialogue that is needed took place in 1979-1980 between representatives of the Women's Ordination Conference and the United States National Conference of Catholic Bishops.[11] The exchange gave hope that the groundwork that has been done is bearing fruit. All of the participants in that dialogue agreed that although the official magisterium of the Church has reaffirmed the traditional exclusion of women from ordained priesthood, "the matter continues to be one of public debate, discussion and ongoing writing and study in the church and in the world."[12]

Conclusion

The question of women in the Church of the future includes but goes beyond the issue of ordination. The deeper question is the recognition of women's full humanity and equality in the church's mission and liturgical life, a recognition that remains to be spelled out in the practical details of church structures and canon law.

The recognition by the representatives of the NCCB that "the alienation of women from the Church is a serious pastoral problem that has many ecclesiological implications"[13] gives hope that the voices that have been raised are beginning to be heard.

But women's real hope lies not so much in the leadership or concessions of the hierarchical church, welcome as these may be, as in the continued grassroots activity of women and men in parishes and in certain circles of scholarship, women and men working toward that ideal of partnership and shared responsibility worthy of those who seek the truth in justice.

The changing position of women in the Church of the future will be a sort of touchstone measuring the extent to which the notion that church structures and practices are historically conditioned and therefore subject to change gains ground over the concept of the divine origin and immutability of these practices. It will be an indication, too, of the extent to which the church as hierarchical institution gives way to the church as people ministering to one another.

The chapter of church history to be written in the coming decade is open-ended. If it is to have a happy ending, women will have to play that part in shaping it which is commensurate with their new awareness and their gifts, with the needs of the Church, and with the demands of justice.

Notes

1. Sr. Albertus Magnus McGrath in her book *What a Modern Catholic Thinks About Women* (Chicago: Thomas More Press, 1972) made an early and important contribution to this analysis.
2. For a good summary of what they describe as the "creative tensions" of feminist theology see the introduction to Carol P. Christ's and Judith Plaskow's *Womanspirit Rising* (New York: Harper Forum Books, 1979), pp. 1-16.
3. Elizabeth Cady Stanton, *The Woman's Bible* (New York: Arno Press, 1972).
4. Naomi Goldenberg, *The Changing of the Gods* (Boston: Beacon Press, 1979), p. 116.
5. Father William Most, "A Guillotine in Rome?" *National Catholic Register*, 31 May, 1981.
6. George H. Tavard, "Sexist Language in Theology?" *Theological Studies* 36 (December 1975): 714.
7. Phyllis Trible, "Eve and Adam: Genesis 2-3 Reread," *Andover Newton Quarterly* 13 (March 1973).
8. Immaculate Conception Church, Elmhurst, Illinois, March 8, 1981.
9. *New Woman, New Church, New Priestly Ministry*. Proceedings of the Second Conference on the Ordination of Roman Catholic Women (Rochester, N.Y., Kirkwood Press, 1980), p. 149.

10. Ibid., pp. 153-154.
11. See "Dialogue on Women in the Church: Interim Report," *Origins* 2 (June 25, 1981): 82-91. This report is an excellent summary of the positions of the two groups in regard to the development of women's full potential in the life of the Church, touching on the questions of personhood, the nature of patriarchy as a social system, and the scriptural, theological, and institutional bases for change in Church teachings and practice.
12. Ibid., p. 91.
13. Ibid., p. 90.

Chapter Six

SCHOOLS

by Edward C. Herr

ONLY America can boast of a unique system of Catholic schools reaching from kindergarten to postgraduate study—a program which more than any other factor accounts for the special characteristics of American Catholicism. No one would argue that Catholic schools are essential to the life of the Church in the 20th century, but it is difficult to conceive of American Catholic life without these schools. Thus the question of whether the next two decades will see the demise or the revival of the Catholic school system in America becomes all the more vital.

To answer this question, I "plumbed" my own experience as principal for 42 years, first in a parish high school and then in a diocesan centralized high school. I contacted personally, and at class reunions, many of the alumni of my graduation classes. I also interviewed over 25 leaders of education in New York, Chicago, St. Louis and Washington, D.C. And I gained an outsider's look at Catholic schools when I accompanied Bishop Albert Ottenweller of the Steubenville (Ohio) Diocese to the Plenary Session of the Pontifical Committee for the Laity which met in Vienna, Austria in July of 1981. These interviews were limited to trends in Catholic elementary and high schools, and were used as background material in this assessment of Catholic Schools in Tomorrow's Church.

Dr. Clement Bezold, director of the Institute for Alternative Futures in Washington, D.C., cautioned me about trying to play prophet: "What would you, in 1957, have imagined to be the future for Catholic Schools?" he asked.

Looking back, I realized that Sputnik (October 4, 1957) radically changed our priorities. James B. Conant, President of Harvard in the Eisenhower years, was calling for centralization of all schools, insisting that no high school have less than 500 students. He demanded that American schools, if they were to compete with Russia's, must put the highest priority on math and science for the next ten years. We American educators—Public and Catholic—*did* just that. Many Catholic schools were centralized. Top priority was given to math and science. Catholic nuns, brothers, and priests packed summer schools and institutes. Enrollment increased and "quality education" became the first order in the Catholic schools of the '60s and early '70s. But even then, in 1964, Mary Perkins Ryan, pointing out that our religious education was not keeping up with our secular priorities, was asking: "Are parish schools the answer?"

As to Dr. Bezold's question, I had to admit that in 1957 if I were looking ahead I would never have

imagined Vatican II, the birth control controversy,
the withdrawal of many priests and sisters from the
priesthood and religious life, the almost total lay
teaching staff in Catholic schools, inflation, high in-
creases in tuition, anti-Vietnam demonstrations, racial riots, or the Supreme Court's decisions on students' rights and on busing for racial integration of
Public schools. But these unpredicted happenings of
the '60s and '70s gradually changed the course of not
only Catholic but Public education as well.

However, Dr. Bezold believes that despite our in-
ability in the late '50s to predict the educational, theological, sociological and racial revolution of the '60s
it is less important today to be right in our predictions than to fail to be imaginative. At its very least
the process of assessing the future will stimulate
readers to become active in helping to shape tomorrow. After all, how many Catholic educators today
remember that Vatican II in its decree on Christian
Education (Oct. 28, 1965), pinpointed an "atmosphere" as the trademark and identification of a
Catholic school?

> Its proper function is to create for the school
> community *a special atmosphere animated by
> the gospel spirit of freedom and love,* to help
> youth grow according to the new creatures they
> were made through Baptism as they develop
> their own personalities, and finally to order the
> whole of human culture to the news of salvation
> so that the knowledge the students gradually ac-

quire of the world, life and man is illumined by
Faith.

One can only speculate what Catholic schools would
be today if Catholic educators of the '60s had focused
on "creating for the school community a special atmosphere animated by the gospel spirit of freedom
and love" instead of math and science.

Keeping in mind, therefore, Dr. Bezold's restrictions on crystal ball-gazing but still recognizing the
value in developing today a creative imagination for
the future, I find the following "givens" on which
most agree. I will then detail two trends which I see
possible in Catholic schools of the future. Which of
these two will predominate will depend upon what
becomes the priorities of the Catholic laity and what
will be the priorities of the bishops, priests, and religious during the remaining years of the 20th century.

Givens

1. There seems to be little doubt that Catholic
schools will continue in America. However, I find
very few young priests, few pastors, few religious—
and evidently few of the American bishops who give
Catholic schools top priority now or in the future. As
for the laity, although some are indifferent and some
opposed, others—admittedly a minority—are willing
to sacrifice time and money to keep their Catholic
schools.

2. Catholic schools today—particularly when compared to Public schools—are providing a "quality"

education, and this should continue in the future. This "given" was augmented by the statistical evidence of the Coleman Report which proved an "Easter Bomb" at the NCEA meeting in 1981 in New York City:

> The evidence is that private schools do produce better cognitive outcomes than public schools. When family background factors that predict achievement are controlled, students in Catholic and other private schools are shown to achieve at higher levels than public school students. [*Overview* Sept. 81—"Catholic Schools"]

3. It is generally agreed that lay teachers will continue to predominate, if not completely staff Catholic schools of the future. With the dwindling of vocations to the priesthood and the religious life, the traditional commitment of nuns and priests in American Catholic schools seems to be over. Admittedly, the sacrifices of the religious orders in America establishing and staffing the Catholic school system made a unique contribution to the history of the Catholic Church. In the heyday of American Catholic schools (1925-1975) the vast majority of priests, brothers, and nuns were committed to fulfilling the Council of Baltimore's decree—"Every Catholic child in a Catholic school"—even to the denial of absolution in the sacrament of penance to parents who refused to send their children to a Catholic school.

4. Catholic school boards will exercise a strong influence in Catholic schools at least in an advisory

capacity. With Vatican II, Catholic schools looked
for a model for shared decision-making and found it
in the Public School boards. The tremendous difference, however, between this model as it was actualized in the parish school boards and in Public school
boards was the power of levying taxes (by vote of the
people) to support the schools. Catholic school
boards, without this force, lack the power base of
their model, and must therefore essentially differ
from their counterpart. The growth of lay Catholic
school boards, however, has increased the determination for keeping these schools open despite a
lack of priority in many pastors' thinking and without the power to control parish subsidies. From this
has arisen the battle for priorities between the parish
council and the parish school board, and the developing controversy over whether the school boards
should be advisory or policy-making. Many feel that
unless these boards are policy-making the laity will
no longer make sacrifices if their efforts are to be
vetoed by the pastor and/or the bishop. Others feel,
however, that the hierarchical structure of the
Church in the future, as in the past, will necessarily
keep boards in an advisory capacity.

5. Finances will be a serious problem for the Catholic schools in the future, as in the present. Many
consider the financial problem to be the most serious
threat and that it must be the schools' primary task to
be answered in the future. Deciding whether Catholic schools should be a parish responsibility as in
the past, or the responsibility only of those whose
children are in Catholic schools, will determine what

will be the shape of Catholic schools in the future. As the tuition rises higher and the enrollment drops lower, the per-pupil cost will increase, and the school may lose its parish and neighborhood identification. Foundations, grants, help from the business community, fund-raising by students, parents, alumni, and boosters, have become and will continue to be part of the financing of Catholic schools. This uniting of teachers, students, and parents in voluntary financing ("earn while you learn") is a unique trademark of American Catholic schools and a frequent target of criticism. But such financing, if tuition is to be kept within reach of the average Catholic parent, is an important substitute for the Public schools' ability to tax-for-finances. As a result, development coordinators in the larger schools are growing into an important part of school administration.

Whether government aid to private schools will become a reality is widely discussed. Most reject direct aid from the government because of the strong probability that Catholic schools would lose their identity—"what Washington finances, Washington controls." The voucher system or tax credits would need a lessening of opposition from the Public schools to succeed. The auxiliary services, bus transportation, text books, and other services to Catholic school *pupils* as distinct from Catholic schools, have been declared constitutional by the Supreme Court and seem unobjectionable to most. But this requires state legislation which many states have refused to pass. With the serious financial problems of Public schools, the financial status of both sectors is now a serious problem.

6. A strong "given" in all discussions is the serious dissatisfaction with the religion "courses" in Catholic schools today. "How *Catholic* are Catholic schools?" is a constant question asked by many parents as more sacrifices are required. They see the breaking-up of the moral fibre of the American family. The divorce rate, the alienation of young people from the parish, the lack of attendance at Sunday Mass affect not only Public school students but also students of Catholic schools. The sexual revolution into which American youth are born today seems to be non-denominational! Many parents say they would make the financial sacrifice if they felt the Catholic school really made a difference. Critical of the content—or lack of content—of today's religion courses and bemoaning the dropping of the Baltimore Catechism without suitable replacement, many parents who would refuse a return to the penalty system, the "guilt complex," the religion-by-memorization of the past, find a scapegoat for today's family upheaval in the post-Vatican II religious education in today's Catholic schools.

7. Demographic studies agree that the moving of the white, upper-middle-class to the suburbs will not be reversed in the future. As Prof. Stephen Bailey of Harvard wrote for *Daedalus* (Summer 1981, p. 38):

At the end of this road, may well be ghettoized schools for the urban poor, non-English language schools for Hispanics, racially pure schools for the bigoted, religious schools for the devout, and for the well-off a whole reversion to the private academies of the 19th century.

Will the Catholic Church of tomorrow be concentrated in the suburbs? Many foresee that the new "minority" Hispanic community (30% of American Catholics are Hispanic) will be the American Catholic majority of the future. As American pluralism becomes actualized in this changing complexion of the American Catholic Church, Catholic schools will undoubtedly be changed. During the late '60s and early '70s the neighborhood ethnic parishes and their schools began to crumble due to the "white flight" and later the upper middle-class "black flight," to the suburbs. Comparatively few Catholic schools followed. If the swing to the "ghettoized schools" means a trend back to ethnic neighborhood parishes as well as Catholic schools, then we may be witnessing another return of the historic pendulum.

With these seven "givens" generally agreed upon, it seems to me that the Catholic schools of tomorrow may very well take either of two roads: The "elite" school or the "Catholic community school." The first would follow the tradition of private schools in the United States and Catholic schools in Western Europe; the latter would carry on the unique and original purpose of the Catholic school system in America. The former would seem to be financially feasible; the latter, as of today, except through the eyes of faith, seem visionary.

"Elite" Schools

In the sixties, after Sputnik, as we said above, most Catholic schools as well as Public schools concentrated on developing a strong math and science program and increased their English and foreign language curriculum. But as the '70s grew older, with the Supreme Court's decisions on student rights and busing for racial integration, Catholic schools became known as leaders in "quality education." At the same time, inflation and a predominantly lay teaching staff forced many to increase their tuition to an extent that they became more exclusive than parish oriented. This development, I believe, may be the trend of Catholic schools in the next 25 years. If that occurs, the Catholic schools in tomorrow's Church will be following the history of European private Catholic schools and not the Catholic school system as we have known it in America.

Spearheading the Catholic Counter-Reformation in the 16th century, St. Ignatius of Loyola and his Jesuits set out to educate the children of the rulers and wealthy classes and developed the Catholic leaders of the next 300 years. These schools became the prototype for highly intellectual and strongly disciplined Catholic education. Countless other male religious orders of priests and brothers, Benedictines, Christian Irish Brothers, Dominicans, etc., established schools, most often separate from parishes. Many of the religious orders of sisters established for girls the same quality educational grade and high schools in Europe and in the United States.

In America this type of Catholic school, although present in the immigrant Church, did not predominate and was often connected with a Catholic college or university. The curriculum of these schools was basically college preparatory. These elite and often exclusive Catholic schools with quality education, strong discipline, and dedicated teachers became associated with the middle and upper classes who have now moved from the cities into the suburbs. And in the inner cities, many Catholic schools in cities such as Chicago, New York, Los Angeles, St. Louis, Baltimore, and Philadelphia have become known for teaching minorities. The proportion of non-Catholic students in these schools was often more than 50 percent. Though the tuition is high—often over $1000—these schools have waiting lists.

In the future, high tuition will be needed to finance these schools with help perhaps from foundations established by alumni—many now in the upper middle and high income classes. Grade schools will continue to be parish centered, but high schools may be regional or connected with religious orders and Catholic colleges. Because of the expense, many comprehensive Catholic high schools may not be able to continue. By and large there will be little place for the poor, the average, and the lower class children who in the past were the bulwark of American Catholic schools.

There are, and will continue to be, Catholic parents who will provide the finances which will be necessary for these schools because they have made a quality Catholic education a necessity for their children. As a result, this type of school will have a select student body and a teaching staff attracted by this exceptional student body, if not by the highest salaries.

The National Opinion Research Center reports that the Catholic schools staffed and administered by religious orders have a strong continuity and tradition and do the best job in developing quality education. Those religious orders which decide to follow the tradition of their founders will continue to make this dedication to Catholic education a high priority. However, because of the lessening of religious vocations and the changing of priorities of most religious orders in the United States from teaching to social or pastoral work, this type of elite Catholic school as it continues will probably be mostly staffed and even administered by lay teachers. Some will be owned by lay groups, organized as non-profit corporations.

The Catholic school boards in future Catholic schools may be policy-making or advisory but will feel responsible not to the hierarchy but to the parents. This type of lay school board will put priority on finances and will insist that the administration be more "business-oriented" than developing as a "faith community."

Strict discipline ("shape up or get out") may well be demanded by parents of the next 20 years who experienced a lack of discipline in their own youth. It was the American nun of the early years who was so convinced that a Catholic education was necessary for upward mobility of Catholics that she was willing —and able—to "pound" knowledge into the students' heads. Perhaps Catholic parents today have worked so hard to give their children the material things which many of them did not have as children that they took little time to hand down to their children the great values that they had received. With the historic pendulum swinging toward conservatism, this type of education may be more popular for the '80s and '90s than it would have been for the '60s and '70s.

The religious education curriculum will be much more content-centered than "experiential." A distinction will be made between the knowledge of the Catholic heritage quantitatively measured and graded, and the practicing of the Faith day by day. Liturgy will be developed for and by children and adolescents, and will be an integral part of Catholic education—retaining the richness of the Catholic heritage and yet related to today's students. This liturgy will arise from these "selective students" through Liturgy Committees under the leadership of musicians, poets, dramatists and theologians, and be the opposite of today's procedure which came from Curial and hierarchical committees downward.

These select students will also have a strong education in the Catholic social message and put it into practice by helping the aged, sick, and handicapped. There is a strong probability that the Third World's influence in the Church will grow and help determine the successors to Pope John Paul II. As a result, a progressive social message and a strong appeal for peace will be generated by these elite schools in the leaders who will graduate from them.

A distinct advantage of these elite schools will be the training of future leaders in America. Perhaps this direction is of the Holy Spirit. Perhaps it will result in a 21st century Catholic Renaissance. John Tracy Ellis' 1950's plea, "Where are the Catholic Intellectuals?" may be answered, "here" fifty years later!

But serious disadvantages will be especially apparent to those of an older generation who have sacrificed to build and staff the American Catholic school system which, as parish-oriented, took in the poor, the alienated, the below average, and the above average students. For the disenfranchised it became the means of upward mobility. In a democracy and a pluralistic society such as America, it seems tragic to think of tomorrow's Church reverting to the "private academies of the XIX century." American Catholicism—different from the Church in 19th century Europe—was not an elite Church. Are we to abort a Catholic school system which took care of the poor and average as well as the middle class and serve primarily the privileged few? We may have future Catholic Intellectuals but what of tomorrow's average Catholic?

"Catholic Community" Schools

But another road for Catholic schools can be visioned: the Catholic Community school. This school system (or network) is as "American as apple pie"

with strong roots in the Baltimore Council's command that every Catholic child be in a Catholic
school. With the trend to develop small communities
—each parish a "community of communities"—the
Catholic school, the elementary and if large enough
the high school, would be the center of the parish. Fr.
Andrew Greeley holds that the Catholic school graduate will continue to be the core around which the
Church in America in the future, as in the past, revolves. This core, although quantitatively smaller
than the '50s, '60s and '70s, will be just as important.

If the parishes, territorial and ethnic, become again
the strong neighborhoods of the future as in the early
history of the American Church, they may renew the
high priority of their Catholic schools. They will differ from the "elite" school because the parishioners
will consider the financing of the school as a parish
responsibility and not only the responsibility of those
parents whose children are enrolled in the Catholic
school. Catholic Community schools will require a
vital religious curriculum, an effective faculty, and
bishops, priests and religious who will again see
Catholic schools as primary in parish life. Fr. Albert
Koob, the former noted president of the National
Catholic Education Association, reminded Catholic
priests and people in 1970 (S.O.S. for Catholic
Schools, Holt, Rinehart & Winston, p. 16), that "the
Catholic school system in the United States was established in response to what Catholic leadership
viewed as a crisis"—the fear of the strong Protestant
orientation of the Public school system. The Catholic
immigrants from Ireland, Germany, Italy, France

and Slovak nations before and after World War I were growing up not only in almost complete ignorance of their heritage of faith but also strongly influenced by the values of the Public schools. Is it impossible in the future to do what the hierarchy, religious and parents accomplished in the past when the Catholic religion was "under seige"? It is possible only if, as a century ago, Catholic schools are made the first order of priority. These Catholic Community schools of the future would have effective lay participation on school boards. The faculty would be role models of Christian values for their students. Catholic universities would set up special training schools especially for Catholic school teachers. If Catholic schools were of supreme importance they would receive the contributed services of lay people as they did of religious a century ago. These Catholic Community schools would probably be smaller, and often would be joined together in regional centers. But with the growth of the electronic revolution (Dr. Bezold speaks of the entire Library of Congress being electronically stored in a one-foot box), more use could be made of public educational services as allowed by the U.S. Supreme Court decisions.

How many bishops are actually planning for these Catholic Community schools in the future can be guessed by the fact that land purchased for new parishes of the future is rarely large enough for anything more than a church, a rectory, and a parking lot!

Acting on James Coleman's findings that the students receive more influence from their fellow students than from their teachers, the Community school would be Catholic atmosphere-oriented as demanded by the Education Decree of Vatican Council II in 1965. Whereas we only gave lip service to the Decree in the '60s and '70s as we were concentrating on science and math, these schools would be distinguished from Public schools by putting this "Decree" of an atmosphere of freedom and love into practice.

The importance of priests and religious in these Catholic Community schools would be recognized and, even though smaller in number, their influence and value as spiritual role models would make their vocations and their presence more attractive. They could truly become "sacraments" to these students and these Catholic communities. Pastors, by their emphasis on parish schools, would inevitably inspire their parishioners to do likewise.

Is this concept of Parish Community schools too visionary? Yes, if this type of Catholic school does not become a top priority of Catholic parents and then of the hierarchy. Yes, if the seminaries do not instill this priority in the young priests of the future. Yes, if our religious communities look only to social and pastoral work as their future. It is probably true that today only the most conservative religious orders seem to have any strong commitment to Catholic schools so that the ultra-conservative *The Wanderer*, like Diogenes of old, goes from diocese to diocese trying to find a "real Catholic school."

So, as the Church enters the last decades of the 20th century, it will probably "inch along" as the

people of God on their pilgrim way, answering tomorrow's problems with today's ideals and priorities. (Twenty-five years ago who could have predicted Vatican II? In the next 25 years what will develop from a Vatican III? Or a World War III?) But as
Dr. Bezold insists, by imagining the alternatives facing us, we will receive the grace to make our priorities those that will truly shape the Catholic schools of
tomorrow into the greatness necessary in America
for the Catholic Church of the 21st century.

Notes

As background material, I have interviewed many Cath-
olic and Public school educators and administrators in
Washington, Chicago, St. Louis, Toledo, and also alumni
of Delphos St. John's and Lima Central Catholic. I espe-
cially wish to thank Fr. Paul C. Reinert, S.J., Chancellor,
Fr. Walter Ong, S.J., and Dr. Michael P. Grady of St. Louis
University; in Washington, D.C.: Rev. Robert J. Yeager,
Executive Director, Secondary School Department
NCEA; Dr. Clement Bezold, Director, Institute for Alter-
native Futures; Sr. Suzanne Hall, S.N.D. deN., Executive
Director, Special Education Department NCEA; Dr. James
Keefe, Director of Research, National Association of Sec-
ondary School Principals; Rev. Thomas G. Gallagher, Sec-
retary for Education, USCC; Msgr. Francis X. Barrett,
Executive Director, Department of Chief Administrators,
NCEA; Dr. Mary Angela Harper, Executive Director, Na-
tional Association of Boards of Education, NCEA; Dr.
William Klepper, Trenton State College, N.J.

Chapter Seven

MARRIAGE

by Mary G. Durkin

CRYSTAL BALL-GAZING is, at best, a risky business. Add to this the task of forecasting the possible directions in the Catholic Church, an institution that remained static for four hundred years, and then, through the initiative of an "interim" Pope, was catapulted into the twentieth century, and the ball grows a bit hazy. Throw in the call to predict what will happen to the institution of marriage, indirectly touching on that most complex of human experiences— sexuality—and the ball becomes positively opaque.

Twenty-five years ago someone hoping to forecast what marriage would be like in the 1980s for Catholics would have felt little compunction about the task. A look at the Catholic position on marriage since the Council of Trent along with consideration of the Code of Canon Law would have given the predictor a sense of the Catholic position on marriage. He or she would then predict a fairly unchanging continuation of this position.

Those of us who married in the 1950s know how confident we felt about what our marriages would be like. And we also know how "off base" we were in our expectations. American Catholics have radically

changed their attitudes on a variety of marriage related subjects—birth control, remarriage after divorce, pre-marital sex, male-female roles, working
women, sexual intimacy, abortion and others. Although the official Church position on many of these
issues has not changed, its new understanding of an-
nulments, responsible parenthood and women's role
in society, to name but a few topics, would not have
been foreseen 25 years ago.

Even with this disclaimer to protect myself, I have
to admit that the only way to predict the future of
marriage for American Catholics is to consider "the
signs of the times" and then imagine what things
would be like if any or all of these signs persist. What
is different about this now, as opposed to earlier
times, is the recognition that there will undoubtedly
be a pluralism in the experience of marriage in the
future of American Catholicism. This will be an acknowledged pluralism. The signs of the times in the
past could have been read as pluralistic, but the important "sign" of the Church's position seemed so
unpluralistic to most American Catholics that it only
allowed for one view of marriage.

This examination of the future of marriage will
consider the pluralism of the "signs of the times"
both in the secular society and in the Church. We
will consider the major Church trends regarding
marriage and what might happen if one of these
trends would receive a greater emphasis from
Church leaders (the unpredictability of these leaders
complicates our task since their decisions will deter-

mine how similar the official Church and laity will be in their views on marriage). We will then be in a position to consider a positive hope for marriage in the future of the American Catholic experience.

Signs of the Times

In all fairness to those of us who did so poorly in our earlier predictions, we have to admit that there have been many changes in attitudes toward marriage in our society. These changes have had both positive and negative significance for the possibilities of marital relationships. They have led to a questioning of old understandings of marriage, understandings developed in response to societal and individual needs no longer as important as they had been in the past. Five factors are greatly responsible for this changing perception of marriage and are "signs of the times" challenging the Church to consider what it has to say about an experience of marriage vastly different than the one existing when many Church rules were formulated.

One major "sign of the times" that is increasingly influential for our understanding of marriage is the change in demographic conditions. We are in a demographic situation where infant mortality rates are down and life expectancy is up. People marrying in their twenties can expect to have fifty years of married life—a fact virtually unheard of at the beginning of the century and unimaginable up until the late eighteenth century when industrial and technological developments led to increasingly better health care and longer lives.

In addition, the survival of more infants has led to a decreased need for women to have many pregnancies to insure the survival of society. Once artificial birth control was perfected to the degree where couples could plan a family and health care offered assurance that offspring would survive to adulthood, the need for women to spend all their child-bearing years in reproducing was reduced, leaving married partners with added years when they would be alone with each other.

When we compare the experience of our grandparents and great-grandparents with our own, we become aware of the vastly different conditions under which a man and a woman live out their marital relationship today. Baring some unforeseen catastrophe which might require a sharp increase in the birth rate, American women will no longer spend their entire adult lives in child-related activities. Spouses will need to relate as more than simply parents of the same children.

This condition will continue to raise questions about life-long commitment. Fifty years of married life, 25 or more of these without the presence of children, changes the nature of a marital relationship. This will cause married partners to question how to be faithful and grow in love and intimacy for 50 years or even longer if the life expectancy rates increase.

A second "sign of the times" is directly related to increased life expectancy. Now that we live longer, we also have more time in which to develop our personalities. Many outside factors influence how that development takes place. Crises of personality growth and development have become a topic of interest most probably because we are experiencing these more acutely than did our ancestors. Not that they might not have had developmental crises, but they would not have had the luxury of being conscious of these or a choice as to how to respond and, in fact, grow in a positive manner.

Personality development confronts married partners with another dilemma which the Church will need to address. Recent studies of life cycles indicate that men and women generally go through particular crises at different times. Gail Sheehey's *Passages*, Levinson's *Seasons of a Man's Life*, Maggie Scarf's *Unfinished Business*, all indicate that marriage partners often experience emotional growth problems that are in direct conflict, thus challenging their ability to grow in intimacy.

Though it is to be expected that there will be some changes in woman's approach to personality growth and development as more and more women consider a career a major component of their lives, there still will be a time in the lives of most women when they will be intimately involved in the child-rearing process. This will undoubtedly continue to affect the way in which women move through some phases of the life cycle though not always as strongly as in the past. It seems reasonable to predict that, even in the future, the crises of growth and development will confront married couples with obstacles to intimacy, obstacles that will force them to look for some "explanation" of why they should continue to strive for an exclusive intimacy relationship for 50 or more years.

A third major "sign of the times," linked with the previous two, is the situation created by the changing role of women and men and new role expectations. Longer life and less years spent bearing and rearing children leave women free to explore other possibilities for the use of their time, energy and talents. They must find meaningful, generative-type activity to fill the time not spent in child rearing (and for those who think this time should most profitably be spent in having large families, the truth of the matter is that few people have the physical or emotional capacity to parent large numbers of children who will live into their adult years).

As women look for new opportunities, they also discover that the long ingrained myths of male and female roles grew out of the need for community survival and for women to reproduce large numbers of children in order to assure that survival. Some women and men today are challenging the stereotypes developed during that period of time, stereotypes which heavily emphasize the man's ability in the world of work and intellectual matters and woman's excellence in caring and nurturing roles. The nature/nurture argument for male and female roles is under close scrutiny, not because we reject physical differences and their possible effects on certain behavior, but because the limits put on the human development of both men and women in order to emphasize these roles are no longer acceptable. The present confusion over what men and women should do to be true to their natures will undoubtedly subside somewhat in the future, but along with it will grow the danger of new stereotypes. We are more comfortable with stereotypes than with the idea that there is a pluralism of approaches to behavior for both men and women.

For now, differing role expectations are causing particular problems. No matter how much we wish to be part of a non-sexist society, we still live in a world where most people were raised in an environment that gave specific roles to men and to women. It will be some generations before the negative aspects of that learning will be eliminated. Conflicts over changing role expectations challenge us to question how it would ever be possible for people who are so different to imagine that they could be happy for an extended period of time in the close intimacy of a marital relationship.

The fourth "sign of the times" grows out of new understanding of human sexuality and the desire for sexual intimacy. In the past, with its strong emphasis on reproduction for survival, sexuality was reduced to concerns about fertility control and erotic behavior, both of which were regulated according to the survival need of the society. Societal attitudes on marriage and family life were strongly linked to religious understandings of the meaning of life in order to support the survival need of the entire family, tribe or nation.

Now that the need for community survival is not pressing, we are beginning to examine the basis of our sexuality and discover the importance of the bonding aspect of our sexual drive, an aspect that the anthropologists and others who study human evolution tell us was essential for the emergence and survival of *homo sapiens*. People now are beginning to expect that sexual intimacy will be satisfying. Magazine articles and books abound telling us how to be sexy. For many of us, the demands for sexual achievement presented in these treatments is as limiting as the previous "rules" of religion. In both the Moral Majority and the *Penthouse* understanding of human sexuality we find a search to understand it "all" with little attention to the need for acquiring the skills of intimacy which might contribute to long range satisfaction in the marital relationship.

Given the confusion evidenced in our society regarding human sexuality it seems safe to predict that there will be a long period of uncertainty about how to achieve sexual intimacy. This situation will often cause turmoil for married people who wish to integrate sexual intimacy into their search for marital satisfaction.

The final "sign of the times" for our discussion becomes apparent when we realize that most Americans hope to find their greatest satisfaction in life through their marriage and family relationship. Given the previous four "signs of the times" it is difficult to imagine how married partners will be able to balance their desire for intimacy, different role expectations, and personality crises over the long years of a marital relationship, and, at the same time, find their greatest satisfaction in this relationship. So it is that this last sign of the times makes us aware of the role that religious imagination and religious vision will need to play in the future of marriage. Only when people's understanding of the ultimate meaning of life encourages them to balance various needs, even when they must give up some of their personal wants, will they be able to work through the challenge of a marital relationship.

In the past, women spent most of their lives in pregnancy and child rearing because they believed it was the will of the gods. Men limited themselves to monogamous relationships so they could provide for the offspring they had fathered (even though they might be tempted to walk away from the situation), because they had formed an emotional bond with their spouse *and* because their understanding of the meaning of life (the story of their gods), encouraged them to do this. Today, and in the future, fidelity will only make sense when a person is able to see it as part of the overall plan for human existence. And this fidelity will require work at developing intimacy on the part of both partners, work that might not even be begun unless the partners have a vision of the meaning of life which inspires them to consider the work a worthwhile task.

So it is that the "signs of the times" concerning

marriage today lead us to predict that in the future American Catholicism will be faced with the task of providing a vision of marriage that will encourage people to make an effort at working at marital intimacy. The vision will need to give reasons for wanting unity with another for committing ourselves to the task of marriage and parenthood for an extended period of time. Only then will people begin to trust their deep desires for unity.

The ability to be saved requires an ability to trust the other who says she loves you. Human nature seems to need this ability if we are to be guaranteed survival. But the need for unity is counterbalanced by the need for individual growth and development. Individual development needs will continually provide obstacles to the need for unity unless some broader perspective on life encourages people to learn how to bring their differences together in some harmonious union. American Catholics, in the future, will continue to need their religious community to offer them a vision that will inspire them in their quest for marital intimacy. We will now examine how the Church might respond to this need by looking at the Church "signs of the times" found in several trends operative in most Church discussions of marriage and marriage related matters.

Church Trends

Regulation Trend. The first trend we will call the Regulation Trend. Let us consider the scene that might occur in the not too distant future if this present trend gains more support among those responsible for official Church positions on marriage:

Bob and Betty are in their early twenties. They have been dating for two years and decide they would like to marry in early June, on the same day that her parents were married twenty-five years ago. Betty receives an engagement ring for Christmas. Shortly after the first of the year they call the rectory to make an appointment for securing the church. Imagine their surprise when they are told it will not be possible for them to marry on the date they had chosen. Recent Church guidelines on marriage have set a nine month waiting period. People responsible for marriage education have become increasingly concerned about the disillusionment that sets in after six months of marriage and have recommended that a couple spend at least nine months being sure about their decision to marry. During this time they are expected to engage in extensive marriage preparation attending a month of "discovery" sessions aimed at weeding out the couples who are mismatched. The hierarchy has been given statistics that indicate that at least two couples out of every twenty that attend these sessions decide not to marry. So, obviously, the sessions are achieving their purpose. They will also meet with married couples of all ages who will give them advice on every aspect of marriage. They will attend a "natural family planning" conference where they will learn how to regulate naturally the number of children they wish to have. The will also receive extensive psychological testing that will show them just where they will be compatible and incompatible.

After all of these conditions have been fulfilled the parish priest will make a decision about whether they are ready to receive the Sacrament of Marriage. In some places they will be told that they are not really mature enough in their understanding of faith to realize the sacramental implications of a Catholic marriage. So a special Church ceremony will be arranged that they will not be held to a sacramental understanding of what is taking place—they will not be entering a sacramental union. Thus, if they should find their relationship incompatible, they will be free at a later time to enter into a sacramental union.

Ridiculous? Preposterous? Impossible? Actually none of this is as far-fetched as it might seem when we consider the regulation trend presently afoot in Church circles. It is interesting how clerically (in the perjoritive sense of that word) oriented some people become when faced with what they consider the enormous responsibility of seeing that all marriages will be successful. People who are extremely liberal in many other areas of Church life suddenly have grabbed on to marriage as a place to show their power. Out of a misplaced concern for the future of the family and the children that might be born to a marital union, as well as concern for the wellbeing of the partners, clergy and laity alike are gravitating toward marriage preparation as the key for assuring happy marriage.

Probably one of the worst ideas to ever come out of
the Cana Conference movement was the thought that
a concentrated course of marriage preparation
would automatically contribute to more successful
marriages (I voice this criticism sure of the good intentions of the Cana movement, having been actively
involved in it for many years, even being part of the
chair-couple of the Chicago conference in the 1960s).
When it appeared that the divorce rate was on the increase, concerned laity, priests and hierarchy, in a
rush to do something about this, decided not only to
continue the pre-Cana tradition but to make it more
elaborate. Thus "guidelines" for marriage which
make the parish priest the arbitrator of who gets married and who doesn't have sprung up in many dioceses.

Unfortunately, even with the best of intentions,
these guidelines often are a hindrance rather than a
help for the Church in its role as provider of religious
vision, especially in the area of marital intimacy. The
"regulators" lack an understanding of the positive
force of romantic love. Attempts to force couples to
face up to their incompatibilities are no guarantee
that when these incompatibilities cause problems in
marital relationships they will be easier to overcome.
In most instances, the discovery of incompatibilities
in premarital discussions will not destroy the romantic illusion built up about a prospective partner, the
romantic illusions which, in fact allow a person to
fall in love despite the obvious shortcomings of the
beloved.

Unfortunately, the guidelines trend, or regulation trend, is catching on. Hierarchy, clergy and laity are, in many instances, supporting the call for guidelines. "It helps to make our ministry more effective," one priest observed. Though many of these people would recoil at the thought that they are on a power trip, these regulators, who are trying to control the beginning of marriage are as much a part of a legalistic understanding of marriage as their colleagues that operate out of the other regulation trend—the Canon Law understanding of marriage.

Even though the easing of the annulment process acknowledges the possibility that every union of two baptized persons in a Church ceremony which has been consummated does not necessarily constitute a sacrament, the Canon Law understanding of marriage still relies heavily on a juridical interpretation of the sacramentality of marriage. Marriage is a contract and as such can be regulated by law. If there is a loophole in the contract, then the contract was not binding in the first place. We are free to break that contract and enter into a new one. Regulators in the Canon Law tradition also try to "control" marriage by tightening up or loosening the interpretation of the meaning of a particular Canon Law regulation.

Unfortunately, though the present annulment procedure acknowledges the possibility that some people never achieve intimacy in a particular marital relationship, most often this acknowledgment does not occur until after one or the other of the marriage partners makes a decision to remarry. The claim that the annulment procedure helps people realize why the first union was unsuccessful and thus avoid making similar mistakes in a second choice is not a valid point. Though at the present time the Canon Law procedure allows some people who have been unsuccessful at achieving marital intimacy in one relationship to attempt a second marital union and still participate in the sacraments, its focus is not on the achievement of intimacy in marriage and the need for religious vision to inspire people in their search for intimacy; rather it views marriage as a legal contract which the Church must control.

Both the guideline and Canon Law regulators of marriage will undoubtedly be influential in the future of marriage in American Catholicism, but only to the degree that married lay people can be convinced there is some validity to these two approaches. An increasing number of lay people, especially the young, are less and less inclined to bother with either the demand to wait a specific length of time before marrying or the requirement to go through an annulment procedure in order to validly remarry in the Church.

Some respond by marrying outside the Church and cutting off all contact with the Church; others marry outside the Church but continue to participate in the sacraments though most often not on a regular basis.

In response to the guideline requirement to wait a specific length of time, many couples are simply shopping around for a priest, parish or diocese that will not hold them to the guidelines. A smaller number of divorced Catholics, who feel that they had a valid reason for terminating their first marriage and still wish to participate in the sacraments after they remarry, are using the "good faith" approach to remarriage; they remarry without the annulment procedure but continue to be actively involved in the Church. There is increasing evidence that even today a large number of Catholics are unwilling to follow "Church rules." There is every reason to suspect that the number of Catholics feeling this way will increase in the future.

Wherever the regulation trend, either in its guideline or Canon Law manifestation, takes hold, we can assume that there will be a gulf between the "official" Church position on marriage and the actual response of lay people to this position. If this should occur on a large scale we predict that the official Church will be unable to respond to the needs of married people—those needs uncovered in our examination of the signs of the times.

Regulations do not lend themselves to the formation of a vision about marriage. When the attention of Church authorities is on regulations, married people will have to look elsewhere for support and encouragement as they deal with the inevitable conflicts of married life. The possible growth of this regulation trend forces us to consider the chance of a not too rosy picture for marriage in the future of American Catholicism.

Vision Trend. An alternative to the Regulation Trend is found in an approach being utilized by some theologians and other observers of Catholic marriage which we will call the Vision Trend. This whole trend has its roots in the belief that religious experience begins in the pre-conscious and that the role of religion and of the Church is to creatively challenge people to discover God's revelation in our preconscious experiences. This approach does not disallow for the possibility of doctrine and even of Church code regarding marriage, but it sees these as outgrowths of the experiences of people's lives rather than as abstract formulations imposed on people. This requires a "grass roots" approach to understanding marriage and cooperation between all levels of Church groups as well as scientific study and conversation between theology and other disciplines. In the midst of such a three-way conversation —between religion, experience and scientific understanding—a vision develops that should inspire and assist people as they attempt to find happiness and God in marital relationships. This trend calls upon people actively to cooperate in the formulation of the vision. They then may respond to the vision and move through the experience of marriage from the perspective of their religious beliefs. The vision trend is actually a call for a spirituality of marital intimacy.

Pope John Paul II in his weekly audience addresses on a theology of sexuality and the body is attempting this approach. His addresses indirectly challenge theologians and others interested in a pastoral vision of marriage to consider how it is possible to put the experience of marriage into an understanding of God's plan for human sexuality. At the present, one of the main problems we have responding to the Papal vision comes from a lack of access to the vision. The audience addresses reproduced in *L'Osservatore Romano* and, for Americans, to be found in the English language edition of *L'Osservatore Romano*, are in a phenomenological and personalistic style that needs to be "translated" into language applicable to the American experiences of marriage. The vision does, however, seek to place an understanding of Christ's view of marriage into a broader understanding of the Divine plan for human marriage as outlined in the beginning text of Genesis where we find that humans were made male and female "in the image of God."

This vision trend will take hold and grow in those areas where pastoral leaders are willing to "let go" of their control of marriage, in those places where pastoral leadership is ready to challenge the religious community to be reflective both about the experience of marriage and about the stories of God we find in our religious tradition. Reflection on the experience of marriage will keep the "signs of the times" and the problems these signs cause for marital intimacy evident during any consideration of a religous view of marriage. This reflection will also uncover the need for a religious vision that will "explain" the Mystery encountered in the experience of marital intimacy. At the same time, reflections on the stories of our faith in light of this understanding of the experience of marriage should lead to an appreciation of the meaning of the Mystery we find in the experience as an expansion of our understanding of our faith. Wherever pastoral leadership is willing to encourage this kind of reflection we can expect American Catholicism to offer a positive vision which will encourage people as they strive to achieve marital intimacy.

Obviously, in light of what we see the "signs of the times" telling us about the future of American marriage, we would hope that the vision trend rather than the regulation trend would influence the future direction of Catholic response to the situation of marriage. If this happens we will be much less certain concerning "exactly" what the future vision will be like. All we can say with certitude is that the beliefs of American Catholics will have a much more profound influence on their married lifestyles if they are offered a vision which grows out of the interaction of their experience and their beliefs.

In summary and conclusion, our crystal ball-gazing has shown us a marital situation that will be characterized by a search for intimacy, a search that will encounter obstacles from increased life expectancy, differences in personality growth and development, changes in role expectations and a desire for sexual intimacy. Without a vision of life that will help balance these various needs, marital partners will find it extremely difficult to remain in a viable marital relationship "until death do us part." The challenge to Catholicism will be the challenge to provide the overall understanding of the meaning of life that will assist in integrating these various needs.

The "signs of the times" in the Church today lead us to predict two possible responses from American Catholicism to the situation of marriage in the future. The regulation response will be less and less satisfying and will contribute to a widening of the gulf between official Church positions on marriage and the experience of married people. The vision response will challenge people to "take charge" of their marital relationship. They will become responsible for contributing to the vision of marriage offered by Catholicism. In addition they will become partners with moralists in developing an "ethos" that will be reflective of this vision.

It would be nice to be able to predict with certainty that the vision trend will predominate but our crystal ball is still a trifle foggy. So we end this reflection on the future of marriage in American Catholicism with the quintessential Catholic attitude: we *hope* that the vision trend will take root and grow.

Chapter Eight

HISPANIC COMMUNITY

by Frank Ponce

IN the large, Cuban-populated Archdiocese of Miami, so the story goes, the crusty Irish pastor heard that numerous French-speaking Haitians were supposed to move into his urban parish. "If they do," he said, "they'd better learn to speak Spanish like the rest of us."

No doubt his answer would have puzzled Solomon and the story is probably apocryphal, but its truth is nonetheless clear. Hispanics in the United States are more visible today than ever before, and their presence in Catholic churches is challenging bishops, priests, sisters and laity—indeed, the entire church—not only to learn the Spanish language but more importantly to embrace (and not merely tolerate) Hispanics as a people whose deep religiosity and rich culture has much to offer contemporary Catholicism.

In the near future, not only will Hispanics be more numerous in the church and in society, they will also be more active in promoting those cultural values which can help bolster institutions like the family, as well as providing those links with the Third World in the Southern hemisphere whence so many came. For Hispanics are here, and they are here to stay.

Indeed, some Hispanics were already here. No other European culture has been in this country longer than the Hispanic; only the American Indian has been here longer. Such an enduring historical presence is one reason Hispanics resent being labeled "foreigners" or "illegal aliens," especially by fellow Christians—who should know better, since in the family of God there are no strangers. A Hispanic Catholic leader, a native New Mexican, pointed to this presence not long ago when he told a conference in Washington, D.C., that for 12 generations his ancestors had lived and died in the same small northern New Mexican town—a history going back to the 1500s. His point? "Hispanics have always lived in the Southwest . . . we, like the Indians, are not interlopers: we are an indigenous people." For in the southwest, Don Juan de Oñate began the colonization of New Mexico in 1595, twelve years before Jamestown and a quarter of a century before the celebrated Pilgrims landed at Plymouth Rock.

The same point about a Hispanic presence could be said about the Southeastern United States. In 1513, Juan Ponce de Leon discovered "La Florida." Forty-two years before the English founded Jamestown in 1607, the Spanish established the first permanent settlement in St. Augustine in 1565. History records that when Father Francisco Lopez de Mendoza Grajalas celebrated the first Mass in America's first city, the sermon was not in English but in Spanish. The purpose of this brief historical excursus is not to lecture condescendingly about the past. Nor is it to romanticize history, for while the Spanish brought the cross they also brought a heavy sword, which in a few tragic years would level the ancient Mayan, Incan and Aztec civilizations and pillage their treasures with a rapacious greed which fed off itself. The "Leyenda Negra" ("Black Legend") of Spanish misdeeds, though exaggerated by hostile (English) writers, will not allow such romanticizing. Rather, it is imperative to stress this historical perspective at the outset for at least two reasons.

One is that doing so may help avoid a repetition in the future of the mistakes of the past. An instance is the attitude of some who assumed they were doing Hispanics a grand favor by accepting them into the United States. History is a difficult taskmaster here, if we but remember the shabby treatment Irish, Germans and others received on first arriving. Can we afford to forget that until a few years ago, both the country and the church were composed principally of immigrants? Hispanics, on the other hand, have a historical identification with this land—especially in the Southwest, much of it once Spain's or Mexico's—which can never be broken and on which they have left their indelible cultural imprint.

Another has to do with the related but distinct question of the function of historical memory. To remember the past is one thing. To remember it as a way of appreciating the present and from it constructing a usable future is another. In a culture whose historical memory is woefully short and where, as de Tocqueville shrewdly observed in the last century, a frenetic mobility blurs and relativizes the many historical contributions of all those groups whose lives helped build this country, it is important for all to know who and what we were and are, as well as what we gave others and received in return. Hence, the historical perspective noted above will help non-Hispanics and Hispanics alike learn from the contributions both have made and continue to make in language, traditions and religious as well as cultural values. But none of this will happen if the very presence of a people or a culture is neither admitted, studied, nor celebrated.

The bishops of the United States took note of this presence in the church when they devoted an entire afternoon's workshop in May, 1980, to a study of Hispanic Catholicism. Archbishop Robert F. Sanchez of Santa Fe introduced the workshop by observing that "just a few years ago very little was said about ministry to the Hispanic," and compared the situation to the biblical passage in which Peter and John ask the Christians of Antioch whether they had received the Holy Spirit, to which the Antiocheans respond that they did not even know there was a Holy Spirit. Then Archbishop Sanchez wryly told his brother bishops: "Perhaps a few years ago if someone had asked us, 'How are you ministering to Hispanics in your diocese?' we might have answered, 'Why, I didn't even know there were Hispanics in my diocese." (*Origins*, Sept. 11, 1980, vol. 10, no. 13, p. 200)

While bishops and others now admit—a few grudgingly—that Hispanics do indeed exist in great numbers in every state of the union, the challenge for the church goes far beyond simply admitting the reality of a large Hispanic presence. What one Hispanic author calls the "Latinization of the United States" is also occurring on a smaller scale as other ethnic, cultural and racial groups arrive in great numbers in the U.S. To be sure, Hispanics from the world's 20 Spanish-speaking countries will continue to come, some to escape poor, repressive or overcrowded homelands for the bright promise of a new life, others to find new jobs and establish a new home for their families. But increasingly Haitians, Cambodians, North Africans as well as refugees from middle eastern countries are flocking here; they bring even greater diversity in language, customs and religions than was thought possible. At issue for the church are not simply the formidable political, economic and social implications of millions of Hispanics coupled with the many thousands of recent (and not so recent) immigrants which will have to be tackled, the sooner the better. The issue rather is how seriously the church will commit itself to living out (and not simply preaching) a healthy pluralism within an ideal of unity that is neither announced nor imposed prematurely. For it will involve the realization that in order to be truly catholic or universal, the church in this country must truly believe that it is good to be different, that not everyone must think, act or dress the same, and that legitimate differences can be ac-

cepted and, again, not merely tolerated. Only thus
will there exist the possibility of expressing in
myriad ways, in many languages and in many cultures, our belief in a loving God and Son who sent
the Spirit at Pentecost to harmonize what Babel dis-
rupted. For humanity's insistence at Babel is that the
City of God is built with a stultifying uniformity;
God's is that the City of Humanity is constructed re-
specting diversity, for God speaks through many cultures and no one should wish to impose the colors of
the sunset on the dawn. This must also be the meaning of Pentecost, where the disciples, gifted with a
universal language, are heard by a cross section of
the world's cultures: "How is it that each of us hears
them in his own native language?" (Acts 2:3-8)

All the more is such an attitude needed today,
when America's rancorous mood accommodates the
recrudescence of the Ku Klux Klan and the anti-intel-
lectualism, self-righteousness and condemnatory
rhetoric of the Moral Majority; a contemporary
writer has said that "whether hatred comes wrapped
in white sheets or the scripture, it is still a denial of
man and his works." Developing such a renewed ecclesial consciousness, especially the need to be one
and yet be diverse, is a perennial task for the entire
church, one which will take on a special urgency in
the near future. And so it is appropriate to ask, how
will the church minister to the needs and hopes of
groups like the Hispanics? Therein lies imbedded another deeper question which will be key in answer-

ing how Hispanics will function in tomorrow's church: will the Hispanics' coming-of-age be seen as a blessing or a burden?

Growth of the Hispanic Population

Many signs already point to the fact that Hispanics are coming of age and will loom large in both the future of U.S. society and the Catholic Church. Numbers are one obvious yet controversial indication. Today Hispanics are the nation's fastest growing minority. This growth also means Hispanics are experiencing rapid changes in the way they live and even where they live. While many may settle in one city for the rest of their lives, for example, others, like Central Americans and Dominicans, may move from one big city to another in search of better living conditions or jobs.

Barely 30 years ago, the 1960 U.S. Census estimated there were 6 million Hispanics. The 1980 Census, the first to count Hispanics directly—previous ones took a five percent sample then made their projections—reported there were 15 million, although even those directing the tabulations admitted there would be an undercount. Knowledgeable Hispanic leaders, who criss-cross the nation and keep in touch with the various Hispanic groups, give a number closer to 20 million. Among other things, what makes the numbers controversial is that no one really knows how many undocumented workers (the so-called "illegal aliens") were uncounted in the census. Estimates as to the number of undocumented workers range from 3 to 7 million, depending on who is using the figures and for what reason.

In any case, the growth of Hispanics has been nothing short of phenomenal. Put another way, while the nation's overall population has multiplied 9 times since 1850, the Hispanic portion has multiplied 147 times and shows little signs of abating. In fact, it is more likely the reverse will happen because in addition to ignoring, for religious and other reasons, zero population ("Hispanics just don't buy it," a population expert remarked when asked why), Hispanics are a young people in comparison with the rest of the population. The median age of Hispanics is 22 years and getting younger; that of non-Hispanics is 32. Of course, especially acculturated Hispanics no doubt also ignore the church's teaching on artificial birth control: perhaps an ongoing *epikeia* helps solve some of the canonical questions.

Small wonder leading secular or Catholic newspapers and journals as well as ecclesiastical and political leaders of every persuasion, all recent "discoverers" of the Hispanic, seldom miss an opportunity to inform a breathless world that the 80s—for good or ill—will be the "Decade of the Hispanic." Former President Carter's 1979 Hispanic Week Proclamation, which presidents assiduously issue every year, noted that today the United States ranks fifth among Spanish-speaking countries of the world. Only Mexico, Spain, Argentina and Colombia have more Hispanics than the U.S. One need only observe life in the great urban centers where 90 percent of His-

panics live to realize the truth of Carter's statement.
New York, Miami, Chicago, San Antonio, El Paso,
Los Angeles and San Diego are in many ways virtually Hispanic cities. Some have Hispanic mayors,
and everything from ads for cigarettes and beer to
metro or bus directions are both in English and
Spanish. There are in many of these cities totally Hispanic barrios, legions of restaurants selling foods,
wines and delicacies as well as Spanish language
newspapers. In Chicago the Hispanic barrio is the
Pilsen area; in Washington, D.C., home for about
75,000 Hispanics, it is Columbia Road. There, and
elsewhere, Spanish is spoken (se habla espanol);
some stores and markets even let you know, lest you
forget: se habla ingles.

A Hispanic Mosaic

But the same Spanish is spoken with an amazing
variety of accents, nuances and idiomatic expressions, for Hispanics are a remarkably diverse people
who rightly resist being lumped together. The word
Hispanic, for example, should not be construed to
mean that the identities of Chicanos, Mexicans,
Puerto Ricans, Cubans, Colombians, Nicaraguans
and others are thus obliterated. The word is simply
an umbrella term used to describe all those people
who come from or are descendents of any of the
world's 20 Spanish-speaking countries. There are
some who argue against its use, insisting instead on
the word Latino, which stresses less the European
Spanish tradition and more the black, Indian and

even Oriental *mestizaje* (mixture). In any case, Hispanic seems to be gaining popularity as the most useful way of speaking about an extremely diverse people, although it must be admitted that to some extent it is a term which the media has legitimized—as it has in past legitimized many other expressions.

Who are the principal components of the Hispanic mosaic? Sixty percent of U.S. Hispanics belong to a group variously described as Chicanos, Mexican Americans, or Mexicans (each term does have a different meaning). Spanish American is another term often used, although its adherents point out that their roots are more from Spain than Mexico. Longtime residents in the Southwest, many Mexican Americans feel that this land, which once belonged to their ancestors, is occupied territory which the United States acquired by force in the brief war with Mexico. With the Treaty of Guadalupe Hidalgo in 1848, Mexico ceded vast lands to the United States, and Mexicans who elected to stay in what was now U.S. territory were guaranteed rights to their land, language and religion. Thousands of Mexicans came to the U.S. during the very bloody and anti-clerical revolution of 1910. Mexican Americans, though found in virtually every state of the union, are concentrated in the states of Texas, Arizona, New Mexico, Colorado and California. New Mexico, which has had a Chicano senator and governor, and now has a Hispanic archbishop, is 48 percent Hispanic; Colorado has 13 percent Hispanics and Arizona over 20 percent. More than 2 million Hispanics of Mex-

ican background live in Texas. With more than 2.5
million Mexicans, Los Angeles—which boasts a Chi-
cana vice mayor—is the largest Mexican city except
Mexico City. By 1985, five million Hispanics will live
in California, giving renewed credence to the
media's so-called "Serape Belt."

Not even a brief account of Chicanos would be
complete without mention of migrant farm workers.
Though mainly Mexican, the farm workers are also
Puerto Rican, black, Central or South American, Fili-
pino and white. Though difficult to enumerate, officials estimate their number at over 1.5 million.
Most are U.S. citizens, though many are also Mexican nationals who are young, male and single. Doing the back-breaking work that puts the fruits of the
earth on the American table, migrant farm workers
travel in season and out, accompanied in many instances by their families, along the "flow" of three
migrant "streams"—the eastern, the midcontinental
and the western. Exploited by farmers and agribusi-
ness, racked by diseases which give them a life expectancy of only 49 years and by lack of educational
opportunities, the migrant farm worker quite often
also lives in poor housing and earns only $4,800 a
year. Today the United Farm Workers of America-
AFL-CIO, under the leadership of its magnetic
founder Cesar Chevez, has made significant strides
in securing basic rights for its members. The support
given by the Catholic Church during the crucial
years of the grape and lettuce boycott, however be-
lated in coming, was nonetheless key in assuring the

union's eventual success. Similar efforts at unioniza-
tion of farm workers are occurring in other parts of
the country, notably those of the Farm Labor Orga-
nizing Committee (FLOC) in the midwest and of the
Texas Farmworkers. Thanks to these efforts and
others, farm workers are among us to stay.

So are more than 1.7 million mainland Puerto
Ricans. U.S. citizens since 1917, Puerto Ricans
began coming to the continent as early as 1910. Like
Mexican Americans, Puerto Ricans are also found in
every state. More than 60 percent live in New York,
but large communities are found in Philadelphia, Los
Angeles, Bridgeport and Hartford, and in many parts
of New Jersey. Puerto Ricans in Chicago already out-
number the white ethnics in formerly Polish, Lith-
uanian and Czechoslovakian neighborhoods. Like
Cubans and other Caribbean peoples, Puerto Ricans
represent a blending of Spanish, black and Indian
cultures. It was the indigenous Taino Indian culture
on the Borinquen island which first introduced
Europeans to products like corn, tobacco and *yucca*.
Puerto Ricans come to the mainland from the crowded island mainly for economic reasons, and this
migration in either direction is a serious sociological
phenomenon which has left its mark and the questions of identity and neo-colonialism. This may be
why the Puerto Rican historian Arturo Morales re-
fers to the "two Puerto Rican communities"—the inner community on the island and the other living
outside of Puerto Rico. It must be remembered that
Puerto Rico was under Spanish influence longer

than any other Spanish American colony, its colonization preceding Cuba's and lasting until 1898. For mainland Puerto Ricans, the choice between an independent Puerto Rico and one that is a commonwealth will continue to add to the tensions involved in living in large crowded Northeast inner cities and in determining where ethnic and cultural identities lie. Because of this and the fact that already Puerto Ricans account for over 17 percent of U.S. Hispanics, they will be increasingly important in the contemporary scene.

The Cubans are the third of the largest identifiable Hispanic groups. Since 1959, when Castro rose to power, over 10 percent of Cuba's population has come to the United States. The Cuban sociologist Juan Clark has written that between 1959 and 1971 a total of 640,000 came to the United States as refugees. With the dramatic arrival in 1980 of over 126,000 Cubans in their desperate flotillas, the number of Cubans in the United States approaches the 900,000 mark. About 50 percent of the Cubans settled in south Florida, especially in Miami. Nowhere is the "Latinization of the U.S." more evident than in "Little Havana" and its environs. Thirty percent of the Cubans settled in the New York-New Jersey area; their presence in this area, coupled with that of Puerto Ricans, Dominicans, Mexicans and others makes possible the argument that New York, not Los Angeles, San Antonio or Miami, has the largest Hispanic population in the U.S. Eight percent of the nation's Cubans are in California, seven percent in Chi-

cago and four in Puerto Rico. Contrary to popular belief, wrote Clark, the Cubans who fled from their
homeland were not all upper or middle class. In fact,
blue collar workers constituted 35.3 percent of the
refugees. On the whole, the work ethic of Cubans has
resulted in high dividends—many own their own
businesses and are exceedingly industrious, yet their
sense of community solidarity has also helped them
succeed; so has their overwhelmingly positive attitude towards the United States, born of gratitude for
being taken into the country. Increasingly articulate,
vocal and active, the Cuban community, now almost
eight percent of the U.S.'s Hispanics, is poised to influence politics in society and in the church.

Nor is this all that can be said about the diversity
among Hispanics. San Francisco is home for considerable Colombians, about 100,000 Nicaraguans and
Salvadoreans plus representatives of 16 other Spanish speaking countries. In New York, three of every
10 Hispanics are other than Puerto Rican. New Or-
leans' large Hispanic population—perhaps 125,000—
is predominantly Central American. As if to under-
score this diversity and intermingling throughout the
nation, the Census Bureau in 1975 reported the following: in Texas, one out of every seven Spanish
speaking persons is other than Mexican American.
In California, one of every four Spanish speaking
persons is other than Mexican American. In Chicago, there are now more Mexican Americans than
Puerto Ricans. In the Pacific Northwest, Washington
State reports the presence of over 80,000 Hispanics,

with similar numbers in Oregon. Most are Mexican Americans and many are migrant farm workers, especially in the Yakima Valley of Washington. And in Miami, one of every four Spanish speaking persons is other than Cuban.

The number, growth and diversity of Hispanics are a reality which society and the church ignore only at their own peril. Ten years ago, except for an occasional newspaper story, Hispanics rarely appeared in the media. If they did, the media inevitably approached them simplistically and played on the preconceptions and stereotypes of those controlling the media and their predominantly non-Hispanic audience. Thus, writes a Chicano expert on the media, "the *Atlantic* headlined a 1967 overview article on Chicanos as 'The Minority Nobody Knows,' indicating that if the existence of Chicanos was news to the editors of the *Atlantic* it must be news to everyone else who mattered." The same thing could be said about *Newsweek*'s 1967 cover story on Hispanics, which called them "this country's best kept secret." Untrue in one sense, the phrase rings true in another. Despite their numbers, Hispanics are still an invisible people. Their existence is relegated to the dusty margins of a dominant white society and their lively popular religiosity has been quickly labeled superstition by a church so steeped in a European ethos its theology and pastoral practice lie in a monocultural rigor mortis. Partially to blame are society's and the church's xenophobic tendencies, and the very real difficulty of managing, in society and the church, the "economy" of accommodation, especially when many groups pursue legitimate interests which will guarantee them the social and religious space necessary to survive as well as build a future.

But at least some of the blame must be laid at the feet of two ideas which have exerted great influence in the shaping of this country. One is the metaphor of the "Melting Pot," described by Sydney Ahlstrom in his magistral *A Religious History of the American People* as that "crucible in which the diverse base metals of the world would be marvelously transformed into pure Anglo Saxon Protestant gold." While social scientists have generally discredited the Melting Pot as a theory (in fact, some write, racial, cultural and ethnic groups, while integrating into society, nonetheless retain much more of their original identity than even they suspect), some political and religious leaders still insist on its validity. While in hot pursuit of this illusory Melting Pot, many have also fallen prey to yet another equally powerful image—America as the Lord's Chosen Nation and the American as the new Adam (or Eve) in a new Eden. Again Ahlstrom writes: "This mythic theme of America as a beacon on a hill and an exemplar for the world became a constitutive element in historical interpretation of the nation's religious life."

What is surprising is not that the Catholic Church should have swallowed these two ideas into its pastoral practice, but rather how long it clung both to the metaphors and their corresponding rhetoric. The phrase "pastoral practice" was used because the church has an impressively profound body of teaching which eloquently defends the right of all peoples to retain their culture in order to facilitate the nurturing of faith. Beginning with Pius XII's defense of immigrants in *Exsul familia* (1952), *Gaudium et Spes'* insistence on a people's "right to culture" (nos. 53-62) and *Ad Gentes'* that ". . . anyone who is going to encounter another people should have a great esteem for their patrimony and their language and their customs" (no. 26), down to Paul VI's famous paragraph 20 in *Evangelii Nuntiandi* (". . . what matters is to evangelize man's culture and cultures (not in a purely decorative way as it were by applying a thin veneer) but in a vital way, in depth and right to the very root") and the numerous references to this question in John Paul II's elocutions and encyclicals (for example, nos. 53 and following of *Catechesi Tradendae*).

That such a rich tradition should have ceded to tawdry statements like "Let them learn English," or "If they want Mass in Spanish let them use the basement and pay for it," not only dramatizes the often shocking disparity between doctrine and practice, but also how very fallibly human we as church can be. Indeed, such statements have often made Hispanics and other groups wonder whether the Church was more interested in Americanizing than in evangelizing, or whether the church has been overzealous in teaching an unquestioned conformity to the American way rather than a Gospel which must be both a personal guide to life and a critic of cultures. What is pellucidly clear today, in any event, is that Hispanics pose an awesome challenge to the church, not as a problem to be solved but as a people to be encountered and loved. For the church the crux of this challenge remains that 90 percent of the nations' 20 million Hispanics are baptized Catholics. Over 25 percent of the church's 50 million Catholics are Hispanic. By the year 2000 that percentage could grow to 49. A crisis? Rather an unparalled evangelizing moment for the church to preach Jesus' Gospel in the midst of a different culture whose values can immeasurably enrich the entire church.

Global Implications: Hispanics and the Third Church

The challenge facing the church, however, is not simply national. It is also global. Due to the growth and influence of Christians and Catholics from Third World countries, in several decades the face of Catholicism on the American continent and elsewhere will no doubt be radically different from what it is today. Father Walbert Bühlmann, à Swiss Capuchin and noted missiologist, has argued that the church's center of gravity is shifting into the Third World. No longer are the important geopolitical poles simply East-West but also North-South; and the situation is weighted in the direction of the Southern hemisphere.[1] Thus, Father Bühlmann states, if birth rates remain more or less constant, the Third Church by the year 2000 will comprise 58 percent of the world's

Christians. Catholics in the continents of Africa,
Asia, Oceania and South America will together
amount to 70 percent of the total number. According
to Father Bühlmann's estimates, some 592 million of
the 854 million Third World Catholics at the end of
this century will live in South America alone. Latin
America, with 44 percent of its population under 15
years of age, is even now home for 40 percent of the
world's Catholics. Need one add that thousands of
immigrants to the U.S. come and will continue to do
so from Mexico and Latin America.

What may all this augur for the U.S. church?

For one, the rapid growth and emergence of Hispanics in the U.S. church (as it were the "Third
Church within") and of Third Churches elsewhere
will call into question an indiscriminate use—at least
in the church—of the word "minority" as a quantita-
tive term; for if Father Bühlmann is correct, in the
year 2000, Catholics from the North will be, not the
majority, but the minority. For another, the challenge
from Hispanics and Third Churches alike will involve for the U.S. church a change in attitude from a
dependence-creating paternalism (maternalism?) to a
liberating trust. The former Apostolic Delegate in the
United States, Archbishop Jean Jadot, signalled the
need for a changed attitude when he told the U.S.
bishops that the pastoral care of minorities was in-
adequate:

> I wonder if the majority of our priests and peo-
> ple realize our shortcomings in these areas and

even our arrogance towards our brothers and
sisters in the faith who are in some ways different from ourselves . . . how are we to give pastoral care to those who do not feel at home with
our white, western European ways of public
worship and community living, to those who
have not adapted and do not want to adapt to
what we call our American way of doing things?
(*Origins*, NC News Documentary Service, vol. 6,
no. 22, Nov. 18, 1976)

If this "arrogance" does exist, perhaps the great challenge of the church in the future is for all its members—first, second, third and fourth world—to adopt
anew a humility which recognizes the legitimacy of
other ways of being and acting, and beyond that, the
essential ineluctable fact that either we are all saved
together or else we perish individually. Doing so may
well teach us humility's greatest lesson, namely, that
it leads to a commitment to pluralism: a willingness
to rise above negotiated self-interests in order to accept both one's own cultural riches and their limitations while reaching out in trust and love to "minorities" like Hispanics, whose cultural values are likewise rich but also imperfect. Such a meeting among
cultures would go a long way toward building solidarity, the genuine exchange involving giving and re-
ceiving which animates pluralism. Indeed, another
word for this experience of pluralism today may well
be solidarity.

Even now Hispanics in the U.S. feel strongly in

solidarity with the hopes and aspirations of their Latin American brothers and sisters. There is a growing conviction, fed by shared experiences, that their destinies are inextricably intertwined, even if their respective situations (especially economic and political) are sometimes vastly different. Nowhere was this solidarity more clearly or forcefully voiced than at the historic *Segundo Encuentro Nacional Hispano de Pastoral* (II National Hispanic Pastoral Encuentro; thereafter, II Encuentro), whose spiritual precursor was the CELAM meeting in Medellin in 1968 and whose organization had affinities with Puebla. It took place in Washington, D.C. in 1977, and was officially convoked by Archbishop Bernardin, then president of the National Conference of Catholic Bishops. The II Encuentro was the culmination of a months-long process which brought together over 1200 Hispanics from across the country, forty bishops as well as numerous local, diocesan, regional and national Hispanic agencies, to carve out a national Catholic Hispanic agenda for the '80s. One of the six Encuentro themes which formed part of the *Proceedings* was "Evangelization and Human Rights." There the delegates unanimously condemned repression in Latin America and spoke eloquently in support of those who defended at great personal risk the human rights "of the poor, the oppressed, the imprisoned, the victimized" (*Proceedings* of the II Encuentro, Secretariat for Hispanic Affairs, NCCB/USCC, Washington, D.C., 1978).

The solidarity between Hispanics here and those in Latin America harken culturally to deep, pervasive blood ties which are often reinvigorated as people from Mexico, the Caribbean and Central and South America filter into the U.S. across man-made boundaries of fluctuating borders, and as U.S. Hispanics journey South eager to slake their cultural thirst in ancestral waters. This bond is sure to grow, making it even more urgent for the U.S. church to determine what will be the nature of its future relationships with Third Churches and elsewhere, and with its own Third Church "within." If recent pronouncements from First World politicians are any indication, the relationship is apt to be increasingly acrimonious and confrontational. It must not be so with the First World Churches, which have much to give and gain from solidarity with the Third Churches, and conversely far too much to lose if such unity and cooperation does not occur.[2]

Hispanics in the U.S.: A Bridge Between North and South?

There are encouraging signs not only that the church is willing, but eager, to construct those bridges of understanding and solidarity with its own Hispanics and beyond that, to Latin America. Eleven years ago the U.S. hierarchy could not point to a single native-born Hispanic bishop. Then on May 5, 1970, Patrick Flores was named the first Hispanic bishop in the history of the United States. Today he is the archbishop of San Antonio and there are 12 other Hispanic bishops. They have journeyed to Latin America to meet with their brother bishops in Riobamba, Ecuador; twice they have hosted meetings of Latin American bishops in the United States. In November, 1980, a diocese in Southern California with a non-Hispanic-bishop (but whose staff has often worked in Latin America), was host to a historic first: a meeting between bishops of the Philippines and Latin America; several U.S. Hispanic bishops were participants. The Northeast Pastoral Center in New York City has its annual meeting of diocesan directors of Hispanic offices in different Caribbean countries, whence many of their people come. The exchange deepens religious and cultural ties, further fostering mutual cooperation in pastoral projects. The prestigious Mexican American Cultural Center (MACC) in San Antonio (whose creative, dynamic president, Father Virgil Elizondo, is one of the few Chicano theologians with a national and international reputation) is a mecca for Liberation theologians who visit, lecture and share pastoral insights they can later take back to their respective countries. Not a few of MACC's students have reciprocated, and indeed, MACC also helps the U.S. bishops train missionaries for service in Latin America. Several dioceses in California, the midwest and the northeast regularly send Hispanics to institutes in Mexico, Colombia, the Dominican Republic and Puerto Rico. The intention is not to duplicate here what is found there, but to foster a mutual exchange, deepen religious bonds and continue an ecclesial dialogue.

Dioceses have responded, too. In 1972 only 25 out of 170 U.S. dioceses had some kind of office to serve Hispanics. Today there are over 120 such offices. The *Comunidades Eclesiales de Base,* brought here from Latin America (and described by one bishop at Puebla as "the theology of liberation put into action"), have existed among Hispanic Catholics here since 1973. Over 1200 of them exist, and they are effective in concienticizing, evangelizing and forming adult Hispanics into pastoral agents. Many non-Hispanics are now asking Hispanics to help form these Basic Christian Communities among their own people. Several dioceses in the West, Southwest and Midwest now have schools for Hispanic lay ministry—*Escuelas de Ministerios Laicales* —to train Hispanics to minister among their own, as is their right, especially where the few Hispanic priests, sisters and deacons cannot do so (the vocation situation among Hispanics is serious though there are some hopeful signs). There are six regional Hispanic offices helping to coordinate pastoral activities in the regions (Far West; Northwest; Southeast; Midwest; Northeast; Southeast) and the dioceses within their area. Most also have a pastoral institute and mobile teams ("equipos moviles") to promote pastoral activity. In addition, several national Hispanic Catholic organizations exist to help support Hispanics in ministry. PADRES is for Hispanic and non-Hispanic priests, and Las Hermanas for Hispanic religious and lay women. Together with the National Spanish Cursillo, *Movimiento Familiar Cristiano* (CFM), an active national Hispanic youth movement, a nascent Hispanic Marriage *Encuentro* and many other efforts too numerous to list here, Hispanics are galvanizing into active, articulate and knowledgeable Catholics who are not simply asking the church to do things for them; they are themselves doing them.

Helping to coordinate many of these efforts nationally is the NCCB/USCC Secretariat for Hispanic Affairs in Washington, D.C. Its executive director for 10 years has been Pablo Sedillo, Jr., who is definitely an activist Chicano. Visionary, energetic and politically astute, he is passionately committed to seeing that Hispanics in deed, not simply in word, become full participants in the life of the church he so loves. Much has been done through the Secretariat. Much has also been done by a legion of Hispanics who, though nameless, continue to labor from within the church and from without to assure that Hispanics' faith and culture, inextricably bound up one with the other, remain intact. It is an arduous task, but in the church and society the dialogue has begun. The bridges of understanding leading to reconciliation among non-Hispanics, Hispanics and Latin Americans are being built slowly but inexorably.

Wither Hispanics in the U.S. Church?

Rather than a bridge, perhaps a journey offers the better Christian metaphor with which to frame the question whose answer we are but dimly beginning to discern. A bridge is after all but one stop among many encountered on the journey.

Whither Hispanics in the church? It is not a matter of Hispanics asking for special treatment. Or even of asking for anything at all, though inevitably the querulousness of the way their concerns are expressed may lead some to ask irritably, "What do those people want?"

In this journey of faith, Hispanics yearn only for what others have always wanted: a place in the House of God where they will be welcomed, feel truly at home, *en su casa*, where they can also live as persons destined to live in community—for Hispanics one cannot separate one from the other, since a person (writes Father Elizondo) is intuitively viewed as communitarian. Hispanics do not wish to undertake this journey alone, and thus wish to travel in union with their extended families—parents, grandparents, aunts, uncles, in-laws, cousins ten-times removed, those who have died but live still in memories which animate reality today. For Hispanics realize that in pilgrimage with one's family we can arrive home to meet all of God's family—the Trinity, the Community of Saints, the family of humankind. In this family will no longer exist the senseless divisions separating races, cultures, nations, only a faith that is ultimately transcultural precisely because its many expressions have been enriched by different cultures who have come to see that their common destiny is to be united with the Lord of History who makes all things new.

"What is essential is invisible to the eye." If Exupery's Little Prince is correct, then the journey must also be embodied in hope. Hispanics hope for nothing more than equal access to the fullness of life in a church which they call *nuestra madre,* be it the Virgin of Guadalupe, of *la Caridad del Cobre* venerated by Cubans, *de la Providencia* by Puerto Ricans, or the many other rich forms she takes in Latin America. They hope to venerate Mary, the saints and the Godhead in their language, with their music, using their traditions and rhythms. For countless Hispanics, the Spanish language, reveling in rich poetic images, palpable, real, sensual, is a language of the heart which allows one to dream the unimaginable, envision the unintelligible, picture the unfathomable. Did not Lorca once say of the Spanish gypsies that they are a people "with their hearts in their heads?" Hispanics are as well. Because communication of this sort is indirect. Hispanics hope that others will give time to allow meanings and nuances to become clear. Tillich once remarked that one of North Atlantic people's greatest sources of suffering was their fear of accepting the limitations of time. Perhaps the well-traveled road to the New Jerusalem needs not only the lovely logical mansions of Aquinas, but also the *mysterion tremendum* of Teresa of Avila's tiered castles, the poetic wisdom of Incas and Mayans, the eloquent practicality of a Cesar Chavez. Surely if God is to be imaged in more than masculine gender, does it not make sense to hope that our common journey needs more than one language to tell our stories?

But without love nothing makes sense, and neither does a journey. Hispanics, indeed all of us, are pre-eminently on a journey of love, to the author of love. Each step taken with hate serves the darkness which threatens always to engulf us all. A step taken in love makes the journey, however difficult, bearable. The Hispanic, thankful for God's gift of life ("tenemos vida") (and who can conceive of neither life nor family without *fiesta*), trusts not law but symbols to express definitvely the commitment to God, to others, to the gift of love.

In the *fiesta* life and death, family and friends, joys and sorrows are gathered in the timeless moment of celebration, short time's endless monument to the lyrical beauty of life, created by a loving God to be celebrated by men and women. The fiesta embraces all this, and men and women do so too with the en-folding *abrazo*—that unfolding of arms to embrace what is loved. Our faith compels us to hope that an *abrazo* of love can overcome our egoism, crumble our divisions and release the power of a new Pente-cost. Then each of us—Hispanics and non-Hispanics alike—"speaking in our language" (Acts 2:8), the common language of Jesus' love, can in *fiesta* pro-claim the lordship of Jesus and celebrate the libera-tion of all his people.

What lies in the future for Hispanic Catholics? What lies ahead for tomorrow's church? Only what awaits us all: the challenge to set out mutually on the pilgrimage and follow it to its very end, knowing that it is the journey, not the arrival, that counts.

Notes

1. Walbert Buhlmann, *The Coming of the Third Church* (Maryknoll, Orbis, 1977). See also Gabriel Marc, "The Institutional Church in the Future," *Pro Mundi Vita Bulletin,* no. 82 (5 July 1980) and Frank Ponce, "Spanish-Speaking Catholics in the United States," *Pro Mundi Vita: Dossiers* 12 (January 1981).

2. See the *Concilium* volume 164 entitled "Tensions Between Churches of the First World and the Third World," edited by Virgil Elizondo and Norbert Greinacher (New York, Seabury Press, 1981). Another interesting view is Marie Augusta Neal's *A Socio-Theology of Letting Go: The Role of a First World Church Facing Third World Peoples* (New York, Paulist Press, 1977).

Chapter Nine

THE BLACK COMMUNITY
by Cyprian Davis

AS an historian I have the inveterate habit of looking to the future by regarding the mirror of the past. In responding to the question of where do I see the black Catholic community in tomorrow's Roman Catholic Church in the United States, I cannot help but look back to the eighties of a century ago. In the late 1880s—in 1888 to be exact—a young black man addressed the national convention of the Catholic Young Men's National Union which was meeting in Cincinnati. The fact that he was invited to speak was in itself significant. What he had to say was even more so. Admitting that he had never dreamed that he would one day be addressing such a gathering— he had been born a slave in Kentucky, in 1854—the speaker went on to say that he wanted to speak about the relationship of the Catholic Church and the black race. He informed the gathering that he had begun a newspaper for the purpose of introducing blacks to Catholicism and the Catholic Church to blacks. He wanted the gathering of young men to know that soon a convention of black Catholics would be held and he wanted their support and interest. He then prophesied, "If the work goes on as it has been going

193

on, there will be awakened a latent force in this country."[1]

This black speaker was named Daniel Rudd. The black Catholic newspaper that he established was entitled *The American Catholic Tribune*. It would be published for over a decade, ceasing in 1899. The convention he spoke about would be the first Black Lay Catholic Congress held in January of 1889 in Washington, D.C. There would be four others to follow. The last would be held in Baltimore in 1894.

Daniel Rudd was convinced that the Catholic Church was the great hope for blacks in this country. He lectured on this theme throughout the South and the North. The Catholic Church, he declared, would erase racism in American society. He brought together leading black Catholics in the five congresses. They took his ideas regarding the church and its influence on behalf of the black race and sought to put them into action. They both failed and succeeded. The movement became too radical for some and the congresses ceased. But the tradition of black lay Catholic involvement in the church and on behalf of the church's mission never really died out. Most would say that Rudd's talk about a "latent force" among blacks relating to Catholicism was typical of his optimistic rhetoric. Most would say that there were few concrete results. Still, no one who would examine the steady growth of Catholicism in the black community during the first part of this century and the even more startling maturing of a black consciousness among black Catholics in the wake of the

Civil Rights movement could deny that a latent force was active.

It is my contention that it has always been there and it still is. For this reason, I project a growth in the black Catholic community in tomorrow's church and I would like to suggest some of the characteristics that this black Catholic community will probably have.

As a student of church history I tend to be optimistic about the future of the church. It is part of the genius of Catholicism to survive and grow back even where many autumns and winters of decline and loss have intervened. For Catholics there has been more than one "second spring." As a black student of history, it seems to me that survival is one thing that we, as blacks, do very well. We have not only survived against many odds, but there has been growth and achievement. This history of the black Catholic community in this country indicates that such a survival was possible because of the spiritual wellsprings within black Catholicism itself.

Today black Catholics number a little over a million communicants in this country. One out of every 25 American blacks is Catholic. Two out of every 100 Catholics are black. About a hundred years ago, when Rudd began his newspaper, there were some eight million blacks in this country and some 200,000 who were Catholic. Today with only a million black Catholics in the United States we represent the largest black religious grouping after the Baptists and the African Methodist Episcopal Church, having about the same number as the next largest black Church, the African Methodist Episcopal Zion Church.

In 1960 there were 106 black priests; today there are about 300 priests and some 700 black sisters. In addition, there are today over 200 black seminarians and about 100 black brothers and an equal number of permanent deacons. In a black population of about 25 million, black Catholics are not extraordinarily numerous. And yet, the growth rate has been steady.

On the other hand, when one considers the climate of opinion regarding racial minorities both within Catholicism and within American society as a whole —American Catholicism more often than not seems to have reflected the larger society—when one considers the pervasive mood of *ennui* regarding blacks and black-related issues, when one considers the pessimism now endemic within the black community, it seems rash to project in the future any growth and development for the black Catholic community. Despite all of these incontrovertible facts, I propose to do just this. I do so not just because the Church as mystery is more often than not "the fruit within the seed" but because there are certain factors present today in the black Catholic community that promise fulfillment in the future. In my opinion there are four.

These four factors are the growth of Catholic worship in a black cultural setting, the role of the Catholic schools in the central city, the pastoral development of black Catholic ministers, and the potential of black Catholic intellectual activity. These factors are signs of life. The first and last factors are signs of maturity in the black Catholic and a forecast of creative development.

Black Catholic Worship in Tomorrow's Church

The renewal of liturgy within the Catholic Church following the Second Vatican Council made possible cultural adaptation within the sacred rites. This cultural adaptation has been most noticeable in non-Western cultures. Nevertheless, the pastoral needs of the people in many areas of the West have made all types of development within the traditional liturgical structures possible.

There are several distinct styles of black religious worship that have developed in American Protestantism. The distinctiveness of black worship is usually most evident in music and in preaching. For black Catholics much of the present liturgical development in black parishes is still in what might be called the "derivative" stage. The songs and music of black Protestant Churches have been freely used in black Catholic worship. In the future, however, one can assume that the same cultural creativity that brought about the "Spirituals" and the "Gospel Music" in their wide variety will result in a Catholic liturgical music that retains the richness of the black idiom and the exuberance of its presentation. This type of creativity among black Catholics has, in fact, already begun. It means also that the ritual movements of the Catholic liturgy will also be exploited even further by a people whose sense of rhythmic movement and dance is the mark of their cultural expression. In fact, Catholic liturgy gives an even wider scope for such creativity. The scope that Catholicism can give to Black artistic expression is already evident in the use of African cloth for vestments and in the use of the dance. A fuller realization, it would seem, is yet to come.

The same holds true for the "black preaching style" which has been so effective in black churches from the beginning of this country. This style has been freely borrowed by many black priests with great effectiveness. Here too the "derivative" stage should soon give way to an authentic black Catholic preaching that fits comfortably within the Catholic liturgical context.

Catholic Schools in the Central City

Today over half of the black population in the United States lives in the central cities. Population shifts have changed the racial make-up of the cities and many of the surrounding suburbs. These changes have been significant for the church. Historically, the Catholic Church in the United States was in the main an urban church. Its demographic strength was in the cities. Now these churches and schools that were once the signs of Catholicity in our cities are signs of decay. They must become the signs of a new challenge to grow. This challenge for growth is most apparent in the parish school of our inner cities. Where previously the school enrollment was generally 100 percent Catholic, today the enrollment is largely black or Hispanic and a large proportion of the student body is non-Catholic.

The Catholic schools have taken on a new importance in the black community. Catholic education has a value that is once again appreciated. Parents in the inner city want an education for their children that instills moral and ethical values along with disciplined learning. Religion is seen as a positive good. The real tragedy would be for the church to ignore its traditional role as teacher. Black Catholics even before the Civil War turned to the church to give instruction to their children. Today it is not only black Catholics but the hard-working parents or the struggling single parent in the central city who look to the church for educating their young in knowledge and in virtue. The black community is more often than not willing to pay for this education. Too often it has been the short-sighted policies of local church officials who failed to see the importance of these schools in the inner city. They failed to remember that the responsibility of the church has never been confined to a narrow membership. All people are potentially children of the church.

It is my projection that the continuance of the Catholic schools in the inner cities of our country— staffed often by lay persons as well as religious, staffed by non-Catholics as well as Catholics, staffed more and more by blacks as well as whites—will mean the growth of the church for tomorrow. If this growth is not in numbers, it will be in long-term influence. More and more black children will have had a contact with the Catholic Church that preceding generations never had. This time their contact with the Church will be through the perspective of the black Catholic community. More than this, it can be predicted that the church will survive in the inner cities to the extent that it nurtures its schools.

Pastoral Activity

Tomorrow's church in the black community will have a pastoral activity geared to the needs of the central city. In a particular way the emergence of the permanent diaconate after Vatican II has a special importance for the inner-city church. Permanent deacons have no difficulty being accepted within the black Catholic community. The deacon is an important figure in the black Protestant Churches. This gives him a recognized status in the black Catholic community. In the very area where the numbers of priests and sisters is being cut back, the permanent deacon should supply the lack, first as a minister with a recognized leadership position in the Church and second as a black minister where blacks in leadership positions are sorely needed. The black permanent deacon consequently has a role to play that the white clergy can rarely play. Moreover, many of the men ready for diaconate know their environment and speak the language of the people. They are not aliens.

Black permanent deacons should not only give a new vitality and a new type of leadership in the black Catholic community of tomorrow, they should provide new pastoral approaches. Will the problems of drug abuse, alcoholism, poverty and crime have disappeared tomorrow? The answer is, not without drastic social changes being implemented today. To meet the pastoral needs of tomorrow's church a new agenda must be drawn up for evangelization and social justice. The permanent diaconate can become the solid basis on which the other structures of pastoral activity can be built.

Both men and women in the black Catholic community have a role to play that is very different from the role played by their counterparts in the suburbs and in affluent parishes. Amid these shifting roles of ministry, the permanent deacon in the black Catholic community will be called upon truly to administrate and coordinate the resources of the church and the community. He can do so as he is one of the people and he knows the people and they know him. He will be tough enough to survive.

Vocations

The dramatic decrease of vocational commitment within the church of today leaves us with a question about the role of religious and the place of the clergy in the church of tomorrow. If it is true that in many parts of the world today the church is finding alternatives for Sunday Mass in places where there is no longer a resident pastor, it is also true that the church of tomorrow must still find within itself the power to generate priestly vocations. It is likewise true that the church as a whole must regenerate itself by bringing forth men and women religious who realize in their lives the charisms of Gospel teaching, asceticism, and the fruits of contemplation. If the church is truly holy, then there must be those who incarnate that holiness in poverty, chastity, and obedience. The external realization of such holiness may change, the reality of the charism will not. It is a question of the work of the Spirit.

Vocations are a top priority within the black Catholic community today. They will continue to be in the same community tomorrow. There has been a steady increase in priestly and religious vocations among black Catholics. This increase, it seems to me, will continue. There are three major reasons for this.

Vocations come from the laity. There is a unified wish among black Catholics for more black priests and more black religious. There is a greater sense of the need to nurture vocations. On the other hand, young people need role models. The growing number of black religious and priests provide a greater number of role models for today's black youth than ever existed before. There is also a greater concern for providing that support to black seminarians, postulants, and novices. Efforts are currently being made to provide information and work sessions to prepare superiors and vocational directors within white communities with knowledge about the black community.

In tomorrow's black Catholic community we

should see emerge formation centers and study centers where black seminarians and black candidates for the religious life can study the roots of their own culture and look at theology and the related sciences from a black cultural perspective. This will be possible because of the increasing number of black religious and priests with degrees and professional formation. One of the quiet revolutions of our time is the intellectual growth within the black Catholic community. The full flowering of this growth will not become apparent until tomorrow's church; the seeding time is today.

Not only should this intellectual growth affect the number of vocations by providing centers of all types for black Catholic studies—some of which will be found in university settings and others which will be local community centres, houses of formation, and perhaps even a seminary—but it should increase Catholic participation in the theological discourse of blacks in this country. To date, black Catholics have contributed very little to the formulation of Black Theology. To date, black Catholics have contributed little to the formulation of Black Spirituality. In tomorrow's church such a contribution will be necessary on the part of the American black Catholic community because African Catholicism and West Indian Catholicism will be leading the way.

The Role of Mediation

In tomorrow's church where it is to be hoped the black Catholic community in the United States will have begun to have a greater sense of its own resourcefulness, there will be a reaching out to other black Catholic communities in Africa and in the Carribean. In some respects this contact has already been made through the sojourn of many African priests and religious in black parishes in the United States. There have also been visits of black Catholic clergy to Africa. What one can envisage for tomorrow's church is a sustained contact on various levels but most particularly in terms of study and theological collaboration.

In many ways the black Catholic community can be and should be the link between American Catholicism and churches of the Third World in Africa, Asia, and Latin America. The history and the collective memory of black Americans have given us a bond with the oppressed and the exploited of the Third World. Ancestry and culture connect us with much of it. On the other hand, the Third World will be even more important in terms of global community and global economy. Tomorrow's church will be living in a world of increased tensions between the North/South axis. The church's role will be even more crucial. The position of the American Catholic Church will thereby be ever more ambiguous. The black Catholic community should be a mediating force, a bridge community.

This role of mediation by the black Catholic community should also hold true within the arena of American society. In tomorrow's American society one can foresee an eventual coalition among the various minority groups within this country. Such a coalition is especially important for the Hispanic groups, the native American groups, and blacks. Competition has heretofore prevented such a coalition. The elements of common possession have not been exploited. In terms of a shared history and a shared spiritual heritage, Catholicism binds many of us together—perhaps this is the one factor that does bind us all outside of a common history of oppression and exploitation.

Survival Factor

Orestes Brownson writing in his periodical, *The Brownson's Quarterly Review,* in 1864 foretold with some complacency the future demise of the black race in America. Brownson whom we may honor as the first great American Catholic thinker was also a racist in the 19th-century tradition. His racial theories were perhaps typical of many American Catholics of the time:

> We do not believe the colored races can, starting with equal chances, maintain equality on the same soil with the white race. Slavery abolished, they will soon be crowded out of the southern states as laborers . . . Hemmed in or crowded out by an ever advancing tide of white population, more vigorous, more energetic, and more enterprising, their numbers will diminish day by day, and gradually the great mass of them will have disappeared, nobody can tell when, where, or how . . .[2]

The fact is that 100 and more years after his dire prophecy, the blacks in this country have increased and their position in the life of this country has become more significant on all levels. Brownson knew nothing about the black Catholic community of his day. He had little regard for black worship and black religion. In the end, Rudd's prophecy of a "latent force" among black Catholics was the more accurate. That "latent force" still exists and its potential must still be more fully realized.

Clouds on the Horizon

The one obstacle is the failure of white American Catholics to face their own racial ambivalence. The failure to confess is a failure to convert. Without conversion, the church will be helpless in tomorrow's sharply divided world. And the division will be between the "haves" and the "have-nots." In our own land this gap will separate inner city from suburbs; small town from rural county.

As a result, all ministry will have to cover some aspect of social concern. The Catholic Church has an historic mandate—dating back to subapostolic times —even to the Gospels themselves—to feed the hungry, to visit the prisons, and to preach the Gospel to the poor. To do otherwise is to abandon black and Hispanic youth to drugs, pimps, and crime. It is to abandon the elderly to slow starvation, despair, and violence. Where federal funds are drying up and federal programs are being cut back, the church must (and I believe will) return to the traditional concerns of a Vincent de Paul, a Martin de Porres, and an Adolph Kolping. This means dedicated service. In tomorrow's church new groups and old groups of religious men and women will return to an old ministry with new techniques and strategies. I fear the church will be ineffective with the youth and the hard-core dispossessed unless it draws on its own resources to provide the means not only for Catholic schools but also for day-care centers, health clinics, half-way houses, drug rehabilitation centers, legal counseling services, economic self-help groups, etc.

It means, moreover, implementing on a fuller scale such programs—unpopular though they be—as affirmative action, equal hiring practices, and the placement of blacks and other minorities and women in decision-making positions.

In our own country, tomorrow's Catholic Church will be multi-colored and bi-lingual to an even greater degree than now. Such a situation will demand an even more profound change in mentality among Catholics in this country. The pastoral letter of the American bishops, *"Brothers and Sisters To Us"* (November, 1979), condemned racism as a sin, but there are many indications that Catholics on the parish level fail to see the implications of that sin in their day-to-day lives. The church seems to preach one thing only to have it understood to mean something else. Such an ambivalence, it would seem, will no longer be possible. The global consequences for the church in the entire world would be too serious. Historical necessity will provide the pressure for

American Catholics either to profess their religion with its consequences in terms of social justice or abandon their faith.

Conclusion

In the final analysis, the church's task is not to reflect any earthly society. Rather the church is to be "a sign for the nations," "a sign of unity, reconciliation, and peace." It is in the interlocking relationships of race and culture that the American church has the greatest challenge to fulfill its mission as sign and sacrament. It is in the context of black America that the Catholic Church will finally experience its moment of grace and truth.

Notes

1. Thomas McMillan, "With Readers and Correspondents," *The Catholic World.* 47 (1888), 711-713.
2. Orestes Brownson, "Abolition and Negro Equality," *The Collected Works of Orestes Brownson.* vol. 17. p. 557. Detroit, Thordike Nourse, Inc., 1885.

Chapter Ten

PROTESTANT AND JEWISH RELATIONS

by Martin E. Marty

Generations

OUTSIDE my library door is a gallery of family mementos. Honored among them is a crocheted infant's bib, a gift to our third son. A yellowing note under it informs passers-by on the second floor hallway that a friend sent it from Assisi on the day Pope John XXIII was elected. Today that son is a college graduate working for the church in Cameroun for a year or two. Both at college, now in that work, and in the years ahead he, a Lutheran, will move at ease with Catholicism. Roman Catholics will never be for him "outside the walls." If in his Camerounian village there is to be mission work or medical work, it may as well be done by a Belgian Catholic nun as by a Norwegian Lutheran minister. If the son writes home about such work, he will discuss its motives, techniques, and effects, but will find no reason to talk about which communion was responsible.

During the first session of the Second Vatican Council our family "adopted" two permanent foster children of Mexican-American and hence of Roman Catholic lineage. The boy of the pair, then two or

209

three, is completing college at a state university. The
Lutheran congregation which he has been attending
has been fragmented over synodical scrapes, become
demoralized, and suffers the kind of suppression that
once Lutherans thought Catholics had patented. In
his long distance phone calls he may mention that
now he has chosen to attend Roman Catholic Mass.
The Saturday night hour is more convenient, the
music is good, the priest is pastoral, the spirituality
impresses him. His foster parents, who have always
seen him as "one of the family" do not spend five
seconds wondering whether he is "slipping" from
Lutheranism—back [?] to Catholicism from which
they snatched him?—but instead spend the seconds
in gratitude that he takes devotional life in Christ
with sufficient seriousness to go to Eucharist at all.

Those two family snapshots pose the issue of generations, of who is doing the viewing of Catholicism
today and prospecting for Catholicism tomorrow. In
1959, when I was about eight years older than these
sons are now, my writing career began. One book
was ecumenical history that breathed hope for closer
relations between Catholics and Protestants. I had
time during the reading of galley proof to insert a
half line about the new papal call for a Vatican Council, but surmised that it would at best have a bit to do
with Eastern Orthodoxy, not with Protestantism. So
remote was Rome.

Meanwhile the same year six of us were invited by
Philip Scharper to contribute to a book, *American*

Catholics: A Protestant-Jewish View (Sheed and Ward, 1959). My chapter in it quoted a Protestant historian, a Jesuit dogmatician, and then a second Protestant historian. "There has been created a broad and impassable cleavage in American society which inevitably creates suspicion, if not open enmity." And: "Catholics often have only the vaguest notion of what Protestants believe, how they worship, and what their religion means to them." Finally: "To most American Protestants, the Catholic remains a mysterious stranger in their midst." Having great hopes for theology in those days, I closed the essay with a hope, even a dream. "Were I to state a Protestant 'dream'—*my* Protestant dream—it would be that out of this could come the invitation from a Roman Catholic bishop for . . . sanctioned [theological] exchange." Several years later I, with many others, was enjoying the benefits of a call by one of those bishops, the Bishop of Rome, to a sanctioned Council, and remember being at a service of commemoration for Father Gustave Weigel, S.J., at which the Pope was himself a member of the congregation.

The gap in perceptions between the coming generation, the American majority, which has not a trace of memory of pre-Vatican II Catholicism and our generation, which saw the great transition, is awesome. Whoever looks ahead to tomorrow's Catholicism has to keep in mind how much can happen in but one generation, or, as we learned between 1958 and 1965, in a seven year span. As I look now, I shall try to combine the historical vantage that a professional church historian brings with the fresh view that a generation "which knew not Pius" brings.

Popes

In tomorrow's Catholicism our generations will see the power of popes, not of papacy. Max Weber wrote about the great shift in leadship from the "charismatic" to the "bureaucratic." Add bureaucratic to hierarchical leadership and you have a style that combines business administration with church dogma. In such a combination, it should matter little who governs and guides. The papacy is what matters, and popes come and go. The curia and the paperwork people, who retain great power, should be the determining factors in non-Catholic views of the Church. But for our two generations this is no longer true.

During the Second Vatican Council, which reversed Max Weber's schedule, a Dutch bishop said that one of the great lessons Pope John forced on Pope Paul was this: papal leadership now had to proceed by persuasion, not by coercion. Whereas once a Josef Stalin sneered "How many divisions has the pope?" to express his disdain for the puniness of Vatican political and military power, today the question comes, "How much power does the pope have over the individual Catholic heart?" The age of mass media of communication, with their passion for charisma and their focus on celebrity, combine with other impulses, including the desire for "pastoral" leadership, to provide new opportunities and new tests for popes.

Theologically, theirs is a sacramental power that comes with ordination and elevation to episcopacy and the papal office. Practically, their power comes from the force of their personality, the integrity of their moral leadership, the eloquence of their rhetoric, the passion of their pursuits. In the age of "mass" society and impersonality, the personality of the Pope has never mattered more. So much comes down to one person, someone who can be impotent if the charisma is lacking, and more potent than most predecessors if the world is charmed or compelled by him.

This was evident to the world in the response to a "smiling pope" during his one month tenure. It was more dramatically evident after the assassination attempt on John Paul II. Most of us had adjusted to foreseeing the Catholic world through the John Paul prism, and expected to do so through the rest of this century. When he was felled, suddenly there was trauma in the prospect of change. Where would there be stability? If he would die, would his successor compel the same kind of attention and display the same kind of "magic" that John Paul did? To my son's generation a kind of relativism about doctrinal and practical development came more easily than to my own. To their generation's mind, it is much more likely that optional celibacy or ordination of women will become licit under a different pope. It is only a matter of time, a change of circumstances, the assertion of will by a pope with a different vision of gender and sex and priesthood. Churchly practice is not fixed in cement and needing to be blasted away as it was in our eyes during Vatican II. Everything is fluid and new popes can write in the gel-like surface that history presents them. But popes *will* write, in that relative world, as they did with less effect in the fixed one in which the senior generation grew up.

Hemispheres

The senior generation grew up in the world of Hilaire Belloc: Europe is the faith. The faith is Europe. Catholicism was the religion of Mediterranean and Atlantic peoples. In our thought the Church in Latin American existed, but was not known except for a few outlines: in Colombia it persecuted Protestants, everywhere it was superstitious and exploitative. But it had no personalities, no one in it had names, nothing in it had power over us.

As for Europe, one now sees a dwindling for "tomorrow's Catholicism." There is not and is not to be a "Third Spring" for English Catholicism. A colleague was graphic about the continent: during Pope Paul VI's tenure, the Alps grew. Better to turn the back, to be bemused but not amused by the antics of those wayward Dutch, secularized French, trouble-making Germans. The pope turned a face toward the future, toward the southern hemisphere. Pope John Paul II looks backward fondly and then, presciently, to Poland, "another Europe"—but western Europe and North America are bewilderingly pluralist. A formula: it is easy to be a Catholic where it is hard to be a Catholic, as in Poland; it is hard to be a Catholic where it is easy to be a Catholic, as in America. The Pope has an easy time with Poland, a hard time with America. He, too, turns southward.

With tomorrow in view, that is not a bad direction to turn. World population growth is in the southern hemisphere, and in this generation for the first time in two millennia the Christian majority will be in that southern hemisphere. Africa, we are told, adds 16,000 Christians a day, many of them Protestant and Pentecostal but many others Catholic. Latin America has come alive, is vibrant, and torn. The heroes and heroines of faith are southern hemispheric. Now that Dorothy Day is gone, there are only Mother Teresa of India and Dom Helder Camara of Brazil and their kind to form the gallery of maybe-saints for the younger Catholic of today.

Tomorrow's Catholic policy will be determined more than yesterday's by life in that southern hemisphere. The present Pope "goes more easily" on the questions of priestly celibacy or lay polygamy in Africa than he would in the northern hemisphere. If the priest shortage becomes severe enough, the diaconate will more likely be enlarged in scope, size, and understanding in the southern hemisphere, and women will have a larger role as the line between priest and deacon blurs and fades. Roman Catholicism by its varied stands on poverty and justice in the El Salvadors of the world lingers in the eyes of Protestant and Jewish America far more than does the Italian Catholicism that cannot repeal relaxed laws on abortion. The drama is to the south, and we, the audience, are increasingly being drawn into the plot. Religion in America is very localized, but if there is to be a vision of the globe, tomorrow's Catholicism, beginning day before yesterday, is the window on that larger world.

Ghettos

A quarter of a century ago, Monsignor John Tracy Ellis stamped on the minds of American Catholics and non-Catholics alike the image of the "ghetto." For him it had been a construct and way of life in which Catholics were sheltered from American pluralism and barred from mainstream intellectual life because they had huddled together. Later-coming immigrants, either despised for their Irish brogues or excluded by their continental languages in an English-speaking world, lived in sequestered valleys or segregated wards. The parish made up the boundaries of their world. A nostalgic Garry Wills spoke for millions, no doubt, when he first derided the foolishness of the old ghetto and then remembered that the ghetto was not a bad place to grow up. A carapace, I would say, under which one could gather meanings, a cocoon in which one could experience nurture. But, still, a ghetto.

This meant to Catholics of my generation, not of my children's, that Catholics had missed out on a great deal. They were not at home in the Harvards of 1882, did not write for *Harper's* back then, did not banter with the Howells or Henry James. Mainline culture passed them by. There was no melting pot, and if it seemed as if there was one, Catholicism in its various ethnic clusters and regional varieties, was still a whole "lump" that did not melt.

Tomorrow's Catholics will see better what we are beginning to see today: yes, Catholicism was a ghetto, but so was almost everything else. Of course, there was *the* culture, a core culture, which had Catholics at the margin. Books named *The American Mind* had few Catholic names in the index before World War II. The Jameses and the Adamses did not condescend to would-be Catholic hobnobbers on their Brahmin heights or in Manhattan apartments. True, all true. But newer images of America suggest that the *the* culture was also a ghetto, a carapace, a cocoon. Those WASPs thought the world of tomorrow was theirs, to be modeled after them. One nineteenth century map I own lists America as a Protestant nation and a textbook says the white race was "the normal race." Combine white and Protestant and you "stood on the mountain top of privilege" as Josiah Strong exalted in the 1880s. The vistas were all yours.

Today the world looks at that old WASPily expansive group and sees but one more enclave, one given over uncommonly to provincialism and chauvinism. The windows were mirrors, and the horizons were limited by different styles of ghetto walls, but ghetto walls all the same. And that tiny core culture was surrounded by many non-Catholic ghettos. My Lutheran forebears in the plains states as late as the twenties did not know there was a "twenties." I once asked my parents about the "roaring" of their youth. They did not know John Held and flappers, gin flasks and F. Scott Fitzgerald. College-bred was my father, but his parental home had in it literally one book, an oilcloth bound Bible, plus the *Old Farmer's Almanac* and the regularly-arriving *Wallace's Farmer*. The family was Swiss Lutheran, making up not only a rural ghetto but an apparent contradiction in terms. A few miles north was a county of Czech freethinkers who ran priests out on a rail and did their contacting of the Absolute in lodge halls and benevolent societies. And a bit east were the Swedes, and beyond them the blacks of South Omaha, and north of them Nebraska's few Jews. And *we* were under the Big Sky where there was room for people to meet each other openly. In New York and Chicago and Milwaukee, German Lutherans and WASP Episcopalians were as closed off from Catholics as Catholics were from them, and all were off from each other.

Tomorrow? I do not know how much of tomorrow's Catholicism will remember the peoplehoods of the past, the ethnic lineages, the Babel, the separate histories of Lithuanians and Irish, or even of Catholic set apart from Protestant. Mixed marriage, the media, the movement of time—all these have bearings we cannot fully foresee, though it is hard not to picture continuing erosion. But in the end the ghetto walls do not wholly fall, and the cocoons never completely break open. If religion does not provide sepa-

rate frameworks for meaning and belonging, something else will: the sub-culture of women who go to
wrestling matches, or Sun Cities, or drag strip
racers, or Elvis memorializers. Creative Catholicism
will work to create some sort of protective shelter,
though it be gossamer and ephemeral, if there is to be
nurture and sustenance through the generations.
Some in Catholicism will try to rebuild the ghetto
walls. The world around us is turning tribal, and
Catholics will not likely be left out entirely from the
impulses of ingathering by people who cannot quite
understand or endure "unlike" next to their "like."
The issue, in short, of walls and spaces, shelter and
exposure, will trouble and excite tomorrow's Catholics to the degree that they want to lead more than
private and reminiscent Catholic existences, to the
degree that they want to be communal and public.

Prejudices

Will tomorrow's Catholic know prejudice? Some
professional societies are constantly monitoring the
air traffic in which anti-Catholic sentiment blips,
constantly walking with metal detectors to see if
there are old filings of prejudice around. Of course
there are. They do not strike me as a significant factor in American group life, where the motives for
anti-Catholicism are few. People have to hate, but it
is more convenient to find more and better objects of
hate than today's generally benign Catholics.

So some Bible bookstores sell weird comic books of
patently anti-Catholic outlook? What does it tell us

about America? Only that it is so pluralist and has so much room for kookery that there are also Nazi parties and Klans. So Planned Parenthood in one of its local chapters turns out a godawfully prejudiced pamphlet? That tells how stupid some voluntary bureaucracies and compulsive ideologues can be, and that America is big enough to have room for foolishness.

More important are the evidences of genuine neighborliness, shared lives, intermarriage, natural empathy and sympathy. More important are the polls which show so many other Americans liking Catholics that soon the percentage of the unprejudiced may pass one hundred. That does not mean that all the respondents are unprejudiced, when tested. But it is not without significance that they see themselves as open and caring, whether out of a deep spirit of what Gabriel Marcel called "counter-intolerance" or what cynics would see as wishy-washiness.

Most Americans do not like whiners or take them very seriously. In a world where Southern Baptists and Moral Majoritarians and Hispanics as Hispanics and not as Catholics and Haitians and effete snobs and hillbillies are objects of real suspicion and true hatred, the professional whiners will not win the day. One does not build a society like America's on altruism but on collisions and collusions between groups with their self-interests. Where the spirit of Christ is not formed in generous Protestant hearts, where "doing justly and loving mercy and walking humbly" does not move Jews to care for Catholics, there are other motives to keep the levels of prejudice low. Catholics belong to too many social classes, have too many political outlooks, live in too many parts of town, for them to be the focus of old-fashioned consistent and persistent prejudice. Sorry, Catholics who want to build group life on paranoia about prejudice the people around you will not make it that easy.

Abortions

Let that triumphalist note about America be qualified: what about abortion? What about the Catholic bishops' stand against abortion? What about the lay Catholic pro-life groups? Was it not prophesied that this would be the issue that would separate Catholics from other Americans and cause a breakdown in conversation with Jews and Protestants?

No such luck. Yes, some of the more obtuse civil libertarian groups for five minutes protested that the bishops had no right or business to plead the case for their vision in legal causes having to do with limiting abortions. These were the same groups that ten years before were applauding the bishops for joining them in seeing moral issues during the Civil Rights struggle or the Vietnamese War. Several things have happened since those first reactions. Many Orthodox Jews also allowed that they had problems with abortion on demand. Southern Baptists, many Lutherans, evangelicals, pentecostals, fundamentalists, not a few mainliners and liberals, some Aristotelian atheists started lining up with questions about abortion, questions that often coincided with or drew upon arguments that Catholic bishops used. True, the stridency and inconsistency of some "pro-life" groups drove many would-be sympathizers for cover at a distance. But the scene became blurry. And unfortunately for the bishops, they surrounded their abortion stand with so many pleas for social justice that they became uninteresting to the voluntarist pro-lifers, who would be fanatic on that one cause. And fortunately for the bishops, unlovelier agitating groups on the Protestant right plunged in to the cause and drew most of the fire.

During a decade of debates ahead over constitutional amendments dealing with abortions, there will be room for dust in the air and the eyes, blows below belts in the confusion, banners dirtied and dropped, gouging, and other mild forms of misunderstanding. Many of these will involve Catholics. But by themselves they will not greatly confuse the ecumenical and interfaith scene because the battle lines are not sufficiently drawn.

Choices

My sons will never know and are not likely to be able to stretch their imagination enough to internalize what they can get from books about pre-Vatican II Catholic style. Therefore they take for granted the way in which the key modern theme, choice, has entered Catholicism. A dramatic way to put the shift between generations is this: Catholicism experienced the decline, if not the disappearance of hell. So long as hell was vivid and threatening, church law and practice could serve as goad or barrier, and church sanction as lure. More and more now God is to be loved for God's sake, for love's sake, and not for reasons of threat. Threat limited choice: the pope says . . . the bishop says . . . the priest says . . . the parent says, and one had no choice.

After Pope John Paul II visited America I heard a butcher, a grandfather from Cicero, talk about the change. Yes, his grandchildren were also Catholic. But we had to take what was set before us. The kids take Catholicism a la carte. They pick and choose. Picking and choosing involves questions of Mass participation, remaining faithful communicants at all, choosing a spouse within the fold, choosing how to raise the children or whether and when to have children and by what means. Choosing means getting Catholicism from the Pope or the catechism or Kung or the college chaplain, or from *Psychology Today* or Marriage Encounter or Warm Tingles or not at all.

The leadership generation of Catholicism has, I think, begun to understand this, and knows it at least in heart and gut. What is more difficult is projecting models and styles into which a new generation can walk. Somehow Protestant evangelicals tend to have a patent on this, so far as the young are concerned. They know how to lure, to provide the ordeal that goes with the rites of passage, to enhance the exhilaration of being "born again," of having made a decision for Christ—of choosing. Tomorrow's Catholicism will be busy finding analogues to those appeals, some clues which the Catholic charismatics have at least stumbled upon, even if the consequences of the way they do it alienate many other Catholics. Catholicism must have more options in its repository, and will be reaching for them.

Extremes

Extreme liberal Catholicism is a vanishing force in North America. It lived for a moment after Vatican II in the ephemeral "underground churches." But it existed chiefly to help people make a transition from compulsory and cramping Catholicism to relaxed secularity. It was a sort of way-station. How little do I have to believe to be considered a Christian, a Catholic? How can I get hippier than thou, more secular than thee? But these were entertaining only to upper-middle aged people who had time for one more quick shot at change. *It* was not a style to be passed on to children. They had no Catholic identity crisis because they had little Catholic identity. They may now remain "open" but if they want to be secular, they can do that without benefit of clergy. If they want to be broadly and vaguely religious, they can be ministered to better by therapy groups and the books on airport newsstands than by covert priests with contraband sacramental elements in above ground apartment underground churches.

Some sort of "liberal" Catholicism lives on, of course, in Liberation Theology and identifications with Third World Catholicism. Now and then they erupt in Berrigan-style demonstrations for peace. There will be more calling into question of new economic policies generated by the federal administration of the early 1980s. What effect they have depends on circumstances far beyond the *ecclesia*, in the economy, the international scene. If the system "holds" and begins to work, they will be marginal. If the New Beginning comes to Early Ending and fails, everything will be up for grabs and they may have a new inning.

Extreme conservative Catholicism lives on with a bit more potency. The Pope gives it little direct encouragement, though a selective following of the current Pope provides some charter and impulse. Yet it is hard to picture the world-wide tribalism, seen in Iran, Israel, Ireland, India, and North American Fundamentalism, leading Catholics into retreat from ecumenical and cosmopolitan zones. People huddle into tribal groups and enjoy the sight of their mirrors and the sound of their solipsisms. They take the beauty of group and memory and soil and turn them into idols of the tribe and builders of illusion. Catholicism can generate some such revanchism, and there are traces of it in the right-wing Catholic press, in the inauguration of some ultra-conservative colleges. Catholicism being Catholic, and thus diverse, it should have room for both far left and far right forces, but as of now the bases for tomorrow's Catholic to want to move along with a mass to that right are not as strong as are the impulses of conservative Protestants to do so.

Mainline

Catholicism, then, tomorrow will continue to be typed as "mainline," with all the rights, privileges, and liabilities attendant thereto. Hate organizes better than love, fanaticism attracts more than openness, absolutism focuses more than responsiveness. Life in the mainline is difficult in a world that does not want to encourage toleration for ambiguity or empathy for the voice of others. Catholicism will hear voices that call it away from mainlinity and Catholic pluralism-in-unity or unity-in-pluralism. But the Catholicism we see at the edge of tomorrow has so many constituencies, so many clientele interests, so many styles of Christian confession, that it is not likely to be able to move from mainline to margin, from diversity toward a monolith. That will not make life easy for the leaders of tomorrow's Catholicism, or secure for the followers. But the call of Christ is not only to safe paths in sheltered ghettos, but into a world of myriad needs and opportunities. Protestants following their similar call, and Jews in their reading of the covenant, will find many reasons to differ with Catholics on their journeys, but just as often, there should be common cause.